KIN

Ettore Sottsass

Ettore Sottsass

JAN BURNEY

TREFOIL PUBLICATIONS, LONDON

Published by Trefoil Publications Ltd
7 Royal Parade, Dawes Rd
London SW 6

First published 1991

ISBN 0 86294 155 5

Design by Elizabeth van Amerongen
Cover design by the Armelle Press
Typeset by OTS (Typesetting) Ltd, Caterham
Printed and bound by Database Resources,
Singapore
Manufactured in Singapore

contents

**For Ettore Sottsass
and for Amanda**

heroes of the design century

More that half a century ago, on January 18th 1933, *Punch* published a menacing cartoon. It showed a figure described as an employer seated at a desk. Standing in front of him was a monstrous mechanical man. In the caption the robot is saying, 'Master, I can do the work of fifty men.' The employer replies, 'Yes, I know that. But *who is to support the fifty men?*'

The ambivalent answer to the cartoon employer's question has been the story of the 20th century. Ever since the Industrial Revolution liberated the developed nations from the agricultural economy of scarcity, the prospect of automation has embodied a threat as well as a promise. A threat of mechanised poverty, oppression, starvation and eventually genocide to set against the promise of automated wealth, freedom, plenty and procreation.

As we look back over the 20th century, it is clear that one activity above all others has come to dominate the shape of the machine-made world. Reality in the late 20th century is *designed*, not shaped by use or custom. In this sense it is already correct to call the 20th century the century of design, for design has been its response to the agonised question of the employer in the *Punch* cartoon.

From diffuse and uncertain beginnings design has become the only human activity that can still promise to connect the support of the fifty men robbed of their work by machines to the productive capabilities of the robot. By perpetually extending the mechanical man in the direction of the human economy, the designers of the 20th century created a world that had never before existed in history. They found ways to close the interface between human consciousness and the man-made material world. Where once technology killed, now it fits. Where once the machine was feared, now it is embraced - and both transformations were carried out by design.

That the designers of the 20th century really have connected the necessity of support with the abundance of invention is a proposition that requires little proof. Even the most extravagant interpretation of human needs in 1933 could scarcely have included one tenth of the goods and services whose universal distribution has today been rendered normal by the activity of design. The multifarious inanimate energy slaves of the late 20th century city would have struck the employer of 1933 as a nightmare of implied social support. Fifty robots instead of one! Who could support the 2,500 men thus thrown out of work? Nor would the answer to this question have seemed credible: that tasks would be created that sixty years ago did not exist. These new tasks, and the purchasing power they have created, are the engines that power the expanding universe of design and production today. The symbiotic phenomenon of design and economic life now exists at a level far beyond the wildest dreams of the industrialists of sixty years ago. Design now sustains economic activity. Already, sixty years after that *Punch* cartoon, design has become the key to the new material world that can support fifty times fifty men. Design is the interdenominational networking of form that makes sense of consumption. From the ten-speed racer to the VCR to the cellular telephone to the workstation to the communications satellite, design is the adhesive that binds all to the global economy. In the end it is design that makes the buying and selling of information as intelligible as once was the buying and selling of slaves and cotton.

But if the new role of design as the engine of consumption is as evolutionarily important as this, how are we to understand its individual workings? At the level of production economics, designers seem no more than a human sub-species, like bees, who work without character or individuality. Indeed today, in investment terms, it has become possible to see the whole design profession in this way, but this is a very recent development.

'Design Heroes' is a series about the individuals who shaped this now homogeneous world of post-industrial design. Men and women who did not resemble the stereotype of today's designers, but who nonetheless created their world of present possibilities for them. Although they seldom worked entirely alone, these 'Design Heroes' established themselves as individual talents, rather than as members of packs like today's design consultancies; packs that are identified by strings of names, cryptic initials or acronyms. These interchangeable box-suited ray-ban figures driving BMWs may be quoted on the USM or listed on Stock Exchanges all over the world, but they are not 'Design Heroes', yet. The classification is reserved for those bold individuals who staked out the first claims in the virgin territory that the corporate designer of today is content to methodically comb and recomb.

Who were these prime individuals, the creators of a new genre of creative human being? The question is more difficult to answer than it might appear, not least because it is only in the last few years that the synergetic importance of design and economics has been popularly grasped.

In the 20th century design always existed, but for years it was not recognised as a unitary phenomenon and its practitioners did their work under different titles with different degrees of status. Sometimes what we would call designers today were 'chief draughtsmen', sometimes 'engineers', sometimes 'inventors', sometimes 'craftsmen', sometimes 'artists', sometimes 'amateur constructors'. In fact the best of them were always Heroes if, consciously or unconsciously, they worked to the dictum of Nietzsche: 'Need is not the reason for something to come into existence, it is an effect of what has already come to be.'

This series of short biographies is an attempt to tell, through the lives of a number of great 20th century designers, how the question posed by the *Punch* cartoon was, and is, being answered. The 'Design Heroes' are men and women who somehow and in some way overdrew on the bank of invention, and in doing so revealed something of the inner mechanism of the creative individual under stress and thus helped to define the elusive modern term 'designer'. All these individuals have been chosen because, in widely different ways, their lives and their works deliver the essence of design as a vital human activity.

We know that it was determination, stamina, endurance beyond the call of reason that created the 'Heroes' of exploration; the 'Heroes' of warfare; the 'Heroes' of speed and flight. Design too makes its calls upon determination, stamina and endurance. 'Design Heroes', like all heroes, are individuals who have been beyond the point of reasonable withdrawal. They have suffered for their work and their convictions. They have overstepped the bounds of conventional behaviour in order not to relinquish the creative integrity of their work.

We know from history that it was not science, but design that created the first engines to pump water; the first mechanical tools to lift rock, bore tunnels and bridge rivers; the first ships that could sail against the wind. Design too created the man-made environment and defined the limits of the dreams of what might still be possible within it. 'Design Heroes' is not a series about the great inventors of the 19th century. It is about the generation that grew up with the elements of the modern world; the car, the passenger aeroplane, the spacecraft and the computer. Men like Richard Buckminster Fuller, whose long life encompassed the history of flight and the history of prefabrication. Raymond Loewy, who designed railway locomotives as well as the interiors of NASA spacecraft. Harley Earl, the creator of the surrealistic finned monsters of the post-World War Two American automobile industry. Ettore Sottsass, who worked on the first Olivetti computers before he broke free from the constraints of Modernism altogether and entered a revolutionary new creative world of furniture design. Colin Chapman, who founded a high-performance automobile legend that he used every resource, even forbidden ones, to keep out of the hands of corporate predators until he died. Tom Karen, who turned a three-wheeled van and a defunct sports car prototype into a hatch-back driven by Royalty.

Through the lives and works of designers like these, the series 'Design Heroes' will change our understanding of what those men and women did who truly learned how to make more production out of less work - by design.

Martin Pawley
Series Editor

introduction

Ettore Sottsass Jnr. is a figure who belongs decisively to the twentieth century. His national and geographical origins were determined by the European upheavals of the First World War and the directions of his career as a designer largely defined by the economic and political legacy of the second. In the fifties he gravitated to America, the contemporary mecca of industrial and consumer production and progress, in the sixties he joined the hippy trail to India and became closely acquainted with Pop Art and the Beat generation. During the seventies he was a leading figure in the so-called Radical Design movement and in the eighties, products and projects from Hindu pottery to houses have given form to years of research and discussion about the nature of environmental design.

Sottsass is himself emphatic that there is a fundamental political basis for existence. The son of a passionately political and patriotic father, he has always had an awareness of his own 'political substance' and firmly believes in sociological destinies. By politics, he does not mean the narrow allegiances represented by party tickets but the surroundings, physical, social and economic, that define people's everyday lives. An awareness of how we are pushed and conditioned by these surroundings and the realization that human situations are largely determined by political conditions is essential, he thinks, to real participation in 'the profession that is life'.

This conviction that it is necessary to know how our lives and attitudes are being influenced by political conditions underlies virtually all of Sottsass's design work. Always, it has attempted to draw the attention of the public, albeit indirectly, to these forces. It has asked people to reconsider the scale of values built up by political status systems and suggested other ways of seeing and doing things. Sottsass is the first person to point out that his output, in terms of actual industrially produced objects,has been relatively small. But he insists that it is not necessary to possess his work in order to be affected by it. His designs are philosophical statements or notes; their importance lies in their ability to communicate rather than their success as products. For him, a good design is like the possibility of going to the moon – very few people will have the opportunity to do it but its existence will change the lives of millions.

It is difficult to imagine a non-twentieth century equivalent of Sottsass. Similarly, it is almost impossible to conceive of him working within a non-Italian context. He was a student in the thirties when the Fascists were establishing a cultural programme that was nationalist, imperialistic and isolationist, cutting Italy off from the artistic movements and experiments that were taking shape elsewhere in Europe.The kind of issues that were being debated by designers and critics – whether arches were preferable to beams, for example – represented deeper political and ideological conflicts within Italian society and it was his exposure to such polemics that convinced Sottsass that the events of his life were the result of a specific social and political situation. 'Italian design,' he has said, 'started in the 1930s with the idea that designing is a political – and *moral* – event, in the sense of confronting oneself with society, history and the anthropological state of the tribe.

In thirties Italy design meant involvement with politics and was considered a way of discussing life, of dealing with living in that time and place. It was a means of expressing a sense of responsibility to propose some kind of form for life, an alternative to Fascism's deliberate closure of debate and attempt to impose a single stylistic identity grounded in archaic and

authoritarian principles. The cultural climate of these years from which Sottsass dates the birth of Italian design was difficult, oppressive and presented many conflicts but with these problems came, he believes, a sense of the meaning of design and of designers' intellectual destinies.

The other dominant feature of inter-war Italy which distinguished, or cut it off, from the rest of Europe was its almost total lack of an organized manufacturing industry. Only those things identified by the Fascist regime as state necessities, almost all of them connected with preparations for war, were produced according to some kind of planned system. Naval and aviation equipment, weapons, railway tracks and stock, auto-

15

Benito Mussolini, *Il Duce*, in 1937.

mobiles – the production of the apparatus of conflict was stepped up with obvious intent. Clearly, Mussolini had immediate plans to initiate the aggression that was bound to result from his expansionist, imperialistic policies but such preoccupations do not encourage the flourishing of creative invention. As Sottsass says, 'War doesn't need design.'

With a few exceptions – some electrical goods and the cars produced by Fiat, Alfa Romeo and Lancia – the industrial production of objects for use in the private domain was virtually an unknown concept in pre-war Italy. Serving the needs of the people however, were thousands of craftsmen producing everything from shoes and silks to furniture, ceramics and glass. Hidden in the simplest workshops in the mountains and islands or operating from quite sophisticated, well-equipped premises in the cities, these craftsmen provided goods to satisfy all the needs of everyday life. Most of these products were made by hand with a maximum degree of precision and the existential possibility of what Sottsass calls 'magic intensity'.

Later Italian designers, including Sottsass himself, have retained a vision of the making of things by hand, with skill and love, even when they are working within a large-scale industrial context. Even when 'revved up' with dreams about the future, like motorbike-crazy Joe Colombo who died of a heart attack in the arms of his lover at the age of 41, they cannot renounce the qualities of the past; their nostalgia for the dream woven around the old culture has never left them. The destruction and confusion wreaked on Italy by the Second World War may have reinforced the dream; certainly it contributed to Sottsass's fear of power, authority,

The Caproni 90. This early Italian plane established a new air freight world record in 1930.

moralism and large-scale cultural and social programmes.

Though trained as an architect, Sottsass had only just qualified when war broke out. After the national and personal traumas he had witnessed during 1939-45, he 'could not think of being an architect', able to deal with public institutions, financial bodies, contractors' organizations.

His view of the profession was still, moreover, an intellectualized one, irreconcilable with business practices. Lacking the resources to set up his own practice, he adopted an alternative position, vigorously participating in the contemporary debates about design that were also debates about life and politics.

LA VETTURA PICCOLA PIÙ

B E L L A
C O M O D A
ECONOMICA

1936 cover of *Casabella*, the architectural magazine edited by Giuseppe Pagano, a leading supporter of Rationalism. The government forced the magazine to cease publication in 1943 and Pagano died in prison in 1945.

Sottsass's Agra sofa for Memphis, 1982, with Zambia fabrics by Nathalie du Pasquier.

The future destiny of Italy, no less, was the big theme of these discussions, many of them recorded in the architectural magazines of the period. Though the protagonists had no money, no homes perhaps, though the country was bereft of resources and working factories, everyone threw themselves into the debates with theatrical vigour. Sottsass talks of the 'tons of adrenalin' that was produced by the Italian population as a means of survival in these post-war years. For many workers and craftsmen, it was directed into the transformation of their *botteghe* or craft workshops into small or medium-sized industries. For others, like himself, it was poured into the production of hundreds of books and magazine articles that reflected a need to see design as some kind of statement, more than just a physical presence.

The main reason, Sottsass thinks, for the fervent compulsion Italians, particularly Italian designers, have to discuss as well as to produce and publish is that they see life as a stage play. Centuries of triumphs, invasions, destruction and rebuilding have left them devoid of any certainty about life as a possible, real, trustworthy system. Thus everyone feels themselves to be simply a character in a play and in order to keep up with the

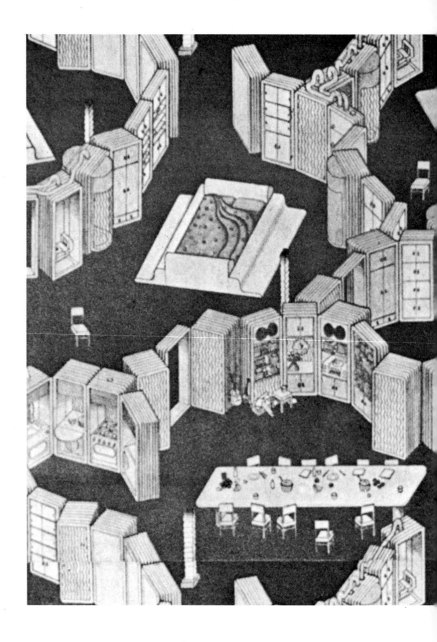

'Micro-environment' designed by Sottsass for 'The New Domestic Landscape', an exhibition of Italian design at the Museum of Modern Art, New York in 1972.

script they must develop their own roles. Facts and reality do not exist, only the play – and it must go on.

Whether the play is a tragedy or a comedy is, says Sottsass , uncertain and it is difficult to be precise about its beginning, plot development and ending. But the important thing for designers is that this performance demands a setting. The supposedly real, solid and eternal natural environment is not suitable for this purpose; such a drama demands decorative, temporary, *emotional* backgrounds and landscapes and the role of Italian design is to provide these backdrops. The devising of stage sets for the happy, sad, romantic, cynical, public and private stories and characters that represent the endless episodes of this dramatic serial of life in Italy is, Sottsass thinks, the driving power behind the whole of Italian industry and design. Since the objects and environments they are creating are simply props for the play, the same importance will be attached to drawings and prototypes as to mass-produced goods.

Sottsass has described how traditional Italian craftsmen shaped by hand objects that would be useful, practical, even enlightening, companions for their possessors' lives. Though their makers were not called designers, they were producing basic communication signs, expressing some vision of how these objects should be used in the enactment of everyday rituals. When the sons and grandsons of these craftsmen adopted mechanized processes, when they returned from their universities to organize and develop small industries with new technology and more sophisticated production programmes, they also realized that industry had to possess and use design. They found, too , that Italy had lots of designers ready to work for them.

Sottsass, returning from America at the end of the fifties, was present at this moment of the dawn of consumerism in Italy. While he had written on the dangers of nostalgia for handicraft as a metaphor for conservatism, he believed that the new objects created by designers should, whatever their means of production, retain the expressive, visionary, ritualistic qualities of their predecessors. His travels in India and a long, potentially fatal illness in the early sixties reinforced

Sottsass's 'Casablanca', finished in plastic print laminate, designed for the first Memphis exhibition in 1981.

his conviction that such objects should contribute to the harmony and symbolism that contemporary western ways of life lacked. Thus in the second half of the sixties he participated in the vision of a young, modern optimistic society in which disastrous social organizations, cultural blackmailing by the government and fear were replaced by an affluent industrial culture. Facilities and diversions like television, hospitals, information, psychoanalysis, sports, music, fashion – and design were now available to everyone and Italian designers now had to shape the stage for this new episode of a happy consumer society.

23

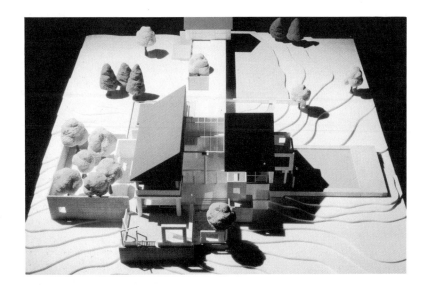

The furniture and objects Sottsass was designing in these years were conceived as essential elements in the rituals of domestic life and at the end of this decade of fast-breeder consumerism – after the revolutionary challenges of 1968 – he was seriously questioning the meaning of a contemporary avalanche of creativity. Environments and objects he designed with other radical groups represented an invitation to imagination, pleasure, awareness and emphasized the idea that design was much more than the combination of beauty and function in a product.

The seventies, for Sottsass, were a period of conceptual preparation. By the end of the period, he was combining the skills and knowledge developed through professional work and research, which he had always practised together, in the creation of objects for Studio Alchymia. The Memphis group, formed in 1981, was the productive symbol and synthesis of years of thought and discussion and at about the same time, Sottsass felt ready at last to establish his own architectural practice, Sottsass Associates.

House in Colorado for the art dealer and collector Daniel Wolf, designed by Sottsass 1986-88.

24

In his own seventies, he now feels 'the possibility of dealing with architecture' culturally and psychologically, as well as having the resources to run an architectural studio. Until now, he has remained 'an intimist, always trying to sort problems not too far from my own body' and he would still be 'desperate' if someone asked him to design a town. But he modestly concedes just a possibility of knowing a bit more now he is older and one thing he and some others are 'slowly beginning to understand' is that there can never be one big totalizing ideology that will solve everything. For that reason, his buildings, like his objects, will express variety, individuality, personal awareness. They will represent the solution to problems one after the other rather than once and for all.

This gradual approach to 'a solution that will never arrive' is typically Italian, thinks Sottsass, pointing to the precedent of medieval and Renaissance towns and cities built around the small-scale elements of piazzas, courtyards, balconies. The creation of settings for the drama of Italian life is clearly safe in such sensitive and comprehending hands but Ettore Sottsass displays an all too clear understanding of the time as well as the place in which he lives. 'Now that we have almost destroyed the planet,' he believes, 'the political power of designers is very small – almost non-existent.' But he adds, 'If we are lucky, we can reach a superficial state of social life, we can try to communicate *something*.' In an age of mass communications and mass confusion, attempts like Sottsass's are more than ever essential.

coming of age in fascist italy

By the time Sottsass embarked on his architectural training at Turin Polytechnic (which, with Milan Polytechnic, was the leading school of architecture at the time) in 1934, the Fascists had been in power in Italy for twelve years, long enough to have established what he calls their 'general catalogue ' of the correct attributes to be exhibited by Italian man. Patriotic to the point of obliteration of self in the interests of his country, his self-image and the one he projected to others should be that of the hero, motivated by a total acceptance of his heroic destiny; any other ideological blueprint was forbidden, out of the question.

The notion of the 'heroic destiny' of the Italian nation was one based on the memory and mythology of the Roman Empire. Everything was organized according to the Fascist version of an imperial Roman state and organizations, attitudes and individuals who appeared to oppose or reject this model were weeded out and brutally castigated for their shamefully subversive tendencies. Any debates concerning not only politics but cultural activities such as literature, art and architecture had to be conducted in an atmosphere of secrecy, usually with a feeling of futility at the impossibility of proposing any alternative to the official Fascist examples.

The Fiat 1500 of 1935, though heavily influenced by American styling, was advertised against a background of Roman ruins to express a new imperialism.

By the beginning of the thirties Fascism had moved towards an increasingly nationalistic and imperialistic stance, antithetical to the apparent spirit of renewal of its first period which was characterized by revolutionary rhetoric. Mussolini himself had been the editor of a radical socialist newspaper, *Avanti*, fond of quoting the 'people's' poet D'Annunzio, and in the late 1920s Fascism still seemed, culturally speaking, a fairly open system. Encouraged by *Il Duce*'s exhortations of the revolution in action and his pronouncements about the need for his regime's support of art, the so-called Italian Rationalist architects had actually succeeded in introducing a modern architectural idiom in Italy. The most prominent group of Rationalists, the *Gruppo Sette*, formed by seven leading modernists in 1926, survived as an active entity for only five years until 1931 but in that time they had gained international recognition for some of Europe's most original and sophisticated examples of modernist architecture.

But by 1935, the year of Italian intervention in Ethiopia, the formation of extreme nationalist and imperialist policies reached its climax. Cultural protectionism swelled to new extremes and Mussolini claimed that, 'The major obstacle to an integration and affirmation of Rationalism in Italy consisted in the incapacity of its theorists to rigorously propose the problem of an antithesis between national and European tastes.' Early urban and international, or 'first hour' Fascism had retreated to retrogressive imperialism and the logical outcome of the new Fascist political doctrine was clearly translated into aesthetics. This is affirmed in Mussolini's new city plan for Rome, scarring the capital's urban fabric, and the over-scaled monumentalism produced in Rome by Marcello Piacentini, president of the Fascist Union of Architects which was given the leader's express sanction to create the regime's official architecture.

Piacentini's stylistic archaeology represented the inevitable architectural expression of the myths on which the seductive attractions of Mussolini's Fascism were based. Purported to be the 'realities' of Italian life to which the Fascist path would lead back, these myths included that of the monumental Mediterranean tradition and the return to order; in a substantially backward nation such as Italy was in the 1920s, this implied no more than a restoration of political and economic privilege, far less any rational organisation of resources.

Detail from a student study of light effects, made at the Turin Academy in 1938.

But for the small, provincial, frustrated and ambitious Italian middle class the mythology exercised a powerful appeal which had led to the defeat of more progressive forces and the triumph of Fascism in 1922

Sottsass was thus too young to participate in Rationalism's first attempt to create an alternative image of contemporary Italy to be projected to the world through its buildings and visual products; by the time he graduated in 1939, almost all the Rationalists had joined the political underground and two leading members of the Gruppo Sette were arrested and sent to German concentration camps where they died in 1945. But he was old enough to be familiar with the most important architectural expressions of their principles. It has sometimes been argued that Sottsass is an anti-functionalist, temperamentally opposed to the 'form follows function' approach to design practised by the architects of the Bauhaus and their followers,

for example. In fact he is, he says, 'very much a functionalist' and it is 'the awful modern, suburban result'
of Bauhaus technological attitudes that he despises and
that has made the surroundings of contemporary towns
so horrible. This is not just the fault of bad architects
but of 'bad politicians and inflexible political mechan-
isms, of rapid population growth and of the problems

arising from the transition of a peasant, agricultural population to an industrial civilisation.' He believes, too, that there has been a widespread and serious misinterpretation of the Bauhaus which applies its functionalist approach only to purely physical problems. Thus it relates everything to the human body, demanding that objects should be nice to touch or easy to work with but ignoring what Sottsass calls the 'more profound functionalism' of the psychological, cultural and political dimension.

He illustrates this notion of different kinds of functionalism with the idea of a chair, perhaps a most beautiful chair, used for different purposes by different people. No matter how beautiful the chair is, it will almost certainly be perceived as uncomfortable by the typist who has been sitting on it for eight hours. If,

A drawing made by Sottsass when he was aged three or four. From earliest childhood, 'Ettorino' had drawn and made things out of any available materials.

ROMA · APRILE - MAGGIO
A · XIII

LITTORIALI
CVLTVRA
ED ARTE

Propaganda of the mid-1930s, extolling the virtues of Fascist art (left). (Below) Marcello Piacentini's project for the Academy of Physical Education in the Foro Mussolini, Rome, 1927-32.

(Above) Giuseppe Terragni: the
Casa del Fascio, Como, 1932-
36 7 and B.P.R. (Belgioioso,
Peressutti, Rogers): Monument
to the victims of concentration
camps, Milan, 1946 (right).

however, the chair has been occupied by someone who sat on it for an hour while awaiting the arrival of their lover, it will be remembered as a comfortable, even a uniquely wonderful chair. The functionalisms, in Sottsass's terms, as related to the worker and to the lover, are different.

Italian inter-war 'functionalist' – or Modern Movement – architecture was also different in visually striking respects, from that of its northern European source countries like Germany and France. Luigi Figini's own house in Milan, built in 1934-35, was strongly influenced by Le Corbusier's Villa Savoye but exhibits the same classical, perhaps Mediterranean, confident and generous elegance as Giuseppe Terragni's Casa del Fascio in Como (1932-36) or Figini and Pollini's Olivetti building of the same period. Such buildings form the nucleus of Italian modernism in design and were responsible for Sottsass's identifying, aesthetically and ideologically, with the Rationalists as opposed to any other group. In addition to his knowledge of their buildings, he also followed the vigorous polemics they carried out in the pages of specialist magazines, particularly *Domus*, whose editor, Eduardo Persico, was Rationalism's major spokesman until he died in 1936, the year that marks the beginning of the retreat of modern architecture in Italy.

Sottsass recalls one event from the early part of this period, around 1930, which illustrates Mussolini's cultural tyranny with regard to architecture. A group of modernist architects in Turin produced a plan for the rebuilding of one of the ancient streets that traversed the city. Lined with glass facades and towers, punctuated with terraces of shops and dramatic lighting, it would have been Europe's most modern street, expressing a Futurist vision of urban life. But Futurism, the influential Italian cultural movement which had flourished from 1909 until the First World War, had already come under censure by Mussolini and his henchmen; internationalist in character, it ran counter to the neo-nationalist tendencies of Fascism and with its rhetorical and actual dependence on the machine, it represented a rejection of the bourgeois social order.

Luigi Figini's own house in Milan, designed with Gino Pollini, 1934-35. Strongly influenced by Le Corbusier's Villa Savoye, it was the first building in Italy to be built on pilotis.

Instead of the optimistic street of the future which, its architects were told by Mussolini, was not in line with the heroic Italian tradition, Turin got a pastiche 18th century style thoroughfare, completed some years later by Piacentini in pure Fascist style. Sottsass relates this incident as an example of how prevailing political and cultural attitudes determined contemporary architectural output and consequently affected the curriculum and activities of the schools of architecture such as his own, at Turin. Any student project even vaguely reminiscent of Bauhaus design or of the work of 'international modern' architects like Gropius or Mies van der Rohe, was considered anti-Fascist, anti-Italian, the product of 'the Judaic-International-Anglo-Saxon Mafia' and a dangerously provocative action on the part of its creator.

The pressures to conform to Fascism's architectural blueprint of monumental historicism, with immense public buildings that would awe and impress the man in the street with the power of the state, determined Sottsass's professional and personal outlook for a very long time to come. Looking back at the thirties and

35

at controversies like the debate, in *Casabella*, about whether a good architect should use arches or beams (Mussolini closed it by declaring that arches, having been invented by the Romans, had to be used in any real Italian architecture) he sees it as the time when design became a problem of giving an image to the process of history.

'To design in Italy in those faraway years,' says Sottsass, 'meant that you had to evaluate your client's morality and to decide how far you wanted to be conditioned by that particular morality or even if you did not want to be conditioned at all.' For many of the Rationalists this lesson was been painfully learnt. Various threads bound individual architects to the Italian political establishment, some being more committed in their support of Mussolini than others. But, in the early years of the movement at least, the desire to build overcame the reservations which some of these young architects may already have been experiencing over the regime's social and moral attitudes.

The Rationalist Manifesto, presented to Mussolini by the participants on the opening day of the Second Exhibition of Rationalist Architecture in Rome in 1931, clearly expresses a wish to be given an opportunity to show what they could do in giving form and image to the Fascist 'revolution'. 'The architects of Mussolini's time,' it said, 'must respond to qualities of masculinity, strength and pride in the Revolution...Our movement has no other moral consequence than to serve the Revolution in hard times. We are asking for Mussolini's faith to give us a way to realize this...To establish an architectural renewal it is essential that we build. We are not asking this for personal gain but rather to express a Fascist idea. Each of us is ready to work for conditions which many of us have relished in action squads.'

There could be no clearer illustration of Sottsass's observation that this was the point in Italian history when designers realized that their role in the drama

Study for a skyscraper in Turin by N. Diulgheroff, 1930, part of a project for a new street by a group of modernist architects. The scheme was dismissed by Mussolini as out of line with the heroic Italian tradition.

(Above and left) Projects for new buildings in Turin by Piacentini, 1935. Instead of a Futurist vision of urban life, Turin got a pastiche 18th century street completed in Fascist style.

of national life was to provide a backdrop for current political performances. The plea inherent in the Manifesto is also evident in the rather vague and cautious language of Gruppo Sette's articles in the magazine *La Rassegna Italiana*. 'We all feel a great necessity for clarity, vision and order,' they wrote. 'Our past and present are not incompatible. We do not wish to ignore our traditional heritage. It is the tradition which transforms its and assumes new aspects.' The desire expressed, to link modernity to tradition, was borne out of a necessary expediency for these young architects. Eager to develop a new Italian vernacular that would provide their country with an architecture as advanced and eloquent as anywhere else in Europe, they had tacitly accepted that the regime's support was essential. Sadly, disillusion was the only possible result of trying to link their ambition with an attempt to gain the patronage of Mussolini's political establishment.

The editor of *Casabella*, Giuseppe Pagano, died in prison; Giuseppe Terragni, the outstandingly talented leader of the Gruppo Sette, committed suicide when he returned from fighting on the Russian Front, unable

The Ansaldo steelworks in Genoa, as seen by an artist c. 1900. Steel production had benefited from government funding since the 1880s. It was essential to the development of the transport systems on which industrial growth, and military expansion, depended.

to come to terms with the horrors of war he had witnessed on that campaign.This was the heroic destiny promised by Fascism, it seemed; architect, designer, intellectual shared the same fate as millions of others, regardless of the specific nature of their professional activities. Design, Sottsass concluded, was not something separate from or above political realities and problems. Rather, it was born out of these and was in a reactive relationship to such occurrences.

At the age of 22, Sottsass, when he graduated in 1939, had no wish to be sent to the mountains to join the fight against France, which was his almost certain fate. In order to avoid or at least postpone it,he sought employment, successfully, as an architect-designer at the Fiat automobile company. He was probably the first designer to be taken on in this industry and was certainly among the very few who were then employed by Italian manufacturers to suggest new and innovative forms for their products. Until then, even the relatively progressive car industry was caught up in what he calls the 'circle game of copies' with German, French, American and Italian manufacturers simply responding to whatever stylistic and technical advances their rivals made with slightly more sophisticated variations on the same theme.

In the north of Italy, particularly in the areas around Milan and Turin, certain industries had benefited from government economic assistance since the last two decades of the nineteenth century. The development of electricity and hydro-electric power had stimulated and encouraged the growth and progress of iron and steel production in these regions; one result of this was a dramatic expansion of the railway system and of the shipbuilding industry. This growth was primarily directed towards military purposes but the manufacture of some 'consumer' goods was also affected by the possibility of factory production offered by new, electric technology and improved iron and steel.

Office equipment produced by the Olivetti typewriter company, founded by Camillo Olivetti in 1908, emerged as one of the new Italian manufacturing industries and during the first decade of the century, bicycle

The Olivetti 'M1' (right) designed by Camillo Olivetti, the first typewriter to be produced by the factory he established in 1908. The Gilera 500cc motor-cycle and sidecar of 1938 (below) was nicknamed 'eight bolts'.

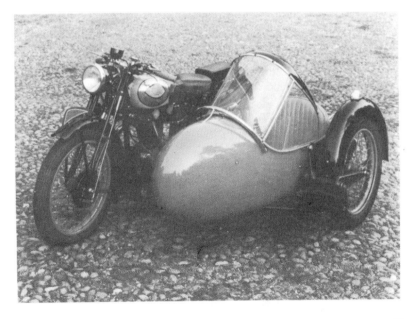

production grew to meet the huge demand for this form of transport which heralded a new mobility for work and leisure. As a form of civilian transport, cars were available to a comparatively small and wealthy minority and Fiat, the first Italian automobile company set up in 1899 produced, like Lancia (1905) and Alfa Romeo (1910), luxuriously upholstered models styled by the craft coach-builders of the railway workshops around Turin. But even before the First World War, Fiat, with the 'Zero' model of 1915, was anticipating the development of mass-produced cars for a wider popular market.

By the 1930s, the automobile industry had been built up into Italy's biggest capitalist enterprise. Even before the First World War, Fiat's founder, Giovanni Agnelli, had visited America to observe mass production in operation in the car industry at the Ford factory in Detroit. Helped by massive government subsidies to stimulate wartime production, the company was sufficiently prosperous by the early twenties to build a huge, ultra-modern new plant at Lingotto where they introduced moving assembly lines and demarcation on the American model. The cars, too, were strongly American-influenced, 1935's Fiat 1500, for instance, echoing the streamlined form of Chrysler predecessors.

U. Dei's 'Impero' touring bicycle of 1937 (above). There was a huge demand for this popular and affordable means of transport. The prototype Fiat 'Zero' of 1911 (right) was designed for mass production at low cost but the need for producing military vehicles impeded prevented any large-scale development.

It was not until the 1950s and 60s that Italian car manufacturing acquired the strong visual identity that emerged from allocating a principal role to design. Classics such as Dante Giacosa's Fiat 500 – the 'Cinquecento', Alfa Romeo's 'Spider' and Ferrari racing cars are a fundamental element in the contemporary image of 'Italian style' but when Sottsass briefly joined the car industry in 1939. he found it 'ignorant, authoritarian and arrogant'. His opinion has not significantly altered in the intervening years and he would still not

Dante Giacosa's Fiat 500 (top), the 'Topolino' (Mickey Mouse) was first manufactured in 1935. The product of innovative engineering and styling, it was cheap to run and enormously popular. The Alfa Romeo 'Spider'(below), launched in the mid-1950s, epitomised sophisticated Italian design.

want to work for such a large and hierarchical organisation. In any case, he was not given the opportunity to extend his disenchantment with Italian industry as he was soon called up and spent most of the war years in Yugoslavia, first as a soldier and later imprisoned in a concentration camp.

post-war projects and polemics

After the war, Sottsass returned to Turin, now perceived by many foreigners as Fiat city, romantic Italy's industrial fringe, usually omitted from the tourist itineraries that swoop from Venice and Verona to Florence and Tuscany, ignoring the urban heartland where most northern Italians live and work. Even those who stop to admire the city's splendid Baroque monuments and elegant arcades may be unaware that Turin, in the twenties and early thirties, was the north's cultural capital, scene of Italy's most advanced art criticism as expounded by writers like Lionello Venturi. It was also the leading centre of political and intellectual resistance to Fascism and home of the socialist philosopher Antonio Gramsci.

More than any other Italian city, Turin possessed a cultural tradition to rival that of the rest of Europe. In the area of art and architecture, its outstanding personalities were the members of *Gruppo Sei* (Group Six), formed in 1928 by the Neapolitan architect, Eduardo Persico and painters from all over Italy and beyond, who included Enrico Paulucci, Carlo Levi, Giorgio Chessa and Jessie Boswell. Several members of the group participated in the Turin Exhibition of 1928, directed by Giuseppe Pagano. The same show provided an opportunity for the city's younger generation of architects to show their work; they included the Swiss Alberto Sartoris, who was to become an important influence on Italian and international architecture, and Ettore Sottsass Snr. who had recently moved to the city with his young family.

Table light by Sarfatti, 1954, typical of the innovative forms of the new Italian design.

47

His father's connections and commitment to modern architecture undoubtedly increased Sottsass's awareness of its struggle for survival in Fascist Italy and , living in Turin, he would certainly have been conscious of the extent to which a cultural and political alternative to Fascism's 'catalogue' existed amongst his father's associates. Because of this early acquaintanceship, the few – but significant – projects that were actually built by the Rationalists would have been known to him even before he became a student of architecture and, with the alternative viewpoint they represented, may have influenced his decision to choose this course.

A few years before Sottsass began his studies, Milan had begun to supersede Turin as the centre of the fight for modern architecture. This was symbolized by Persico and Pagano's move in 1929 and 1930 to the former city where they became, respectively, director and editor-in-chief of *Casabella*. Though a long way from Rome, the centre of government, Milan was to become, most noticeably after the war, the indisputable 'design capital' of Italy and even of Europe. Rome was essentially the administrative city, a filter rather than a destination for interior migration and in 1945 it lacked any tradition of architectural patronage other than in the public sector which was dependent upon political fluctuations. Milan, an industrial city, emerged from the war with a strong reputation for resistance to Fascism and to that regime's attempt to outlaw modern architecture; there was also a rudimentary class of potential patrons of architecture and design amongst its manufacturing and business population.

The Biennale exhibitions of 'Decorative Art' which had traditionally taken place in Monza, were renamed the 'International Triennale of Decorative and Modern Industrial Art' in 1930 and moved to Milan where they acquired a more international flavour, particularly the sixth Triennale of 1936 for which Pagano designed a strikingly rationalistic entrance hall. Persico created the large hall which Vittorio Gregotti has described as 'one of the most remarkable works of Italian architecture of the period...the metaphysical tension of its ghost-like pillars is connected with that classic ideal' and Figini, Pollini, Terragni and other Rationalists built a series of small dwellings in the park surrounding the exhibition buildings.

It was through such exhibitions plus the polemics in the magazines and their coverage of one of the few other outlets for the expression of new architectural ideas, competitions (like the one for Florence Railway Station won by Giovanni Michelucci's group in 1934), that students of Sottsass's generation first encountered modern design. Though the Rationalists had abandoned any ideas of winning the struggle for public approval by 1936, a year of strong anti-modern reaction in Italy as elsewhere in Europe, *Casabella* continued to publish after Persico's death in the same year until the government forced it to stop doing so in 1943. The challenges confronting the next generation had already been made clear in the magazines by observa-

Green and Pink Still Life,
Enrico Paulucci 1929-30 (top)
and *Seated Nude with Red
Fabric*, Giorgio Chessa 1932
(below). The two painters were
members of the *Gruppo Sei*
formed in Turin in 1928. Both
artists participated in the Turin
Exhibition of 1928, where
Ettore Sottsass Snr. also
exhibited some of his
architectural drawings.

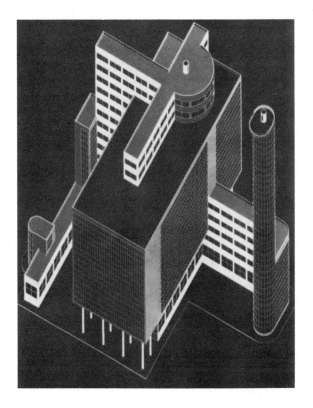

Axonometric of Notre Dame du Phare, 1931, by Alberto Sartoris, a Swiss architect based in Turin who influenced Italian rationalism through his contact with international architecture. Sartoris became the chronicler and historian of rationalism and was also the designer of some experimental modern furniture, exhibited at the sixth Triennale in 1936.

tions like, 'Today the artist must face the most troublesome problems of Italian life: the reliance on set theories and the will to carry on to the very end the battle against the demands of an "anti-modern" majority... Such demands, repudiated by the idealistic stubbornness of Italian polemicists, constitute the heritage that we will leave to coming generations, after having fatally wasted our time with stylistic problems.' (Eduardo Persico in *Domus*, 1934).

When Sottsass returned from Yugoslavia to Turin in 1945 there was little opportunity even to become involved with problems of style. 'I found myself in a country totally destroyed,' he has written, 'with no reason at all, with a very difficult future, with a very confused political and cultural programme... I became

51

more and more scared, more and more horrified by the Carabinieri, by any institution, by power in any form, by any authority, by any crystallized moralism, by any virginity, by any programme that was larger than my arms or slower than the fast river of history.'

Apart from his personal doubts and anxieties, his inability to see 'how my horribly intellectualized vision of the profession could fit anywhere in Italy in those days, how it could fit with the anxious and Mafia-business oriented practicalities of everyday life', there was little for young Italian architects to do in their impoverished and broken country, physically and morally devastated by war and civil war. If, like Sottsass, they had no money or powerful contacts they might turn, as he did, to painting and sculpture.

As his drawings for the interior design examinations at Turin Polytechnic show, Sottsass's ideas about colour and space were greatly influenced by contemporary painters like Picasso and Matisse (whose work he had seen in Paris), Mondrian and Kandinsky. The latter's theories concerning sensual and emotional responses

Cover for the catalogue of the sixth Milan Triennale, 1936 (left) and Mario Sironi's poster for the fifth Triennale, 1933 (right). When the Triennales moved from Monza to Milan in 1933, the exhibitions became the major international showcase for modern Italian architecture and industrial design.

52

to colour and form are clearly echoed in all of Sottsass's creative activities. Surface decoration remains a preoccupation in everything he does and one of the first articles about his work, in the late 1930s, described his ideas about the use of colour as a delineator of space. Since he was a child, Sottsass had drawn, painted and sculpted objects out of wood and clay; while he was in the army he painted portraits and even sketched out textile designs that were printed by the Montenegro craftsmen. When he returned to Turin 'fine art' activities like sculpture and designing book covers occupied much of the time when there was little architectural work available. In 1946, he organized an international exhibition of abstract art, the first in Milan, with Bruno Munari, an artist and designer who had been part of the later Futurist movement.

The Victory Hall of the 1936 Triennale. The hall is one of the most remarkable works of the Neapolitan architect Eduardo Persico, a brilliant critic, director of *Casabella*, and the most controversial supporter of modern Italian architecture. The ghostlike pillars recall the classical ideal, though Persico was opposed to the Milanese neo-classical movement of the time.

R.Camus's gallery of industrial decorative art (top) and Bottoni and Pucci's doctor's waiting room exhibit at the 1936 Triennale. Although that exhibition marked a definite move towards Rationalism, a strong anti-modern reaction emerged in Italy, as elsewhere in Europe, after 1936.

The opportunities for design in a practical sense started to increase when he moved to Milan in 1946. The reconstruction programme had begun and, as an architect, Sottsass was able to participate in the rebuilding projects made possible by Marshall Plan funding. With this assistance, the Government-subsidized INA (National Insurance Institute) Casa programme was established to finance and stimulate an extensive nation-wide series of low-cost housing schemes to improve the inadequate and sub-standard accommodation of most of working class Italy, particularly in the south. Bureaucratic and petty political wrangling conspired against the success of INA Casa but some interesting projects were completed in spite of severe financial and stylistic restraints.

Sottsass is dismissively modest about his architectural work at this time but his workers' housing scheme at Romentino in Novara was considered sufficiently interesting, when it was built in 1951, to be published in *Domus* as were several of the other designs for housing he produced. The influence of Le Corbusier is clear in these but it was enriched with Sottsass's attempt to incorporate vernacular features that he had observed in the rural dwellings of Montenegro and various regions of Italy such as Sardinia and the Po Valley. Open staircases, central piazzas, a brightly coloured decorative lattice screen on the front of an apartment block; Sottsass's housing indicated that he had no intention of limiting his formal approach to a particular set of principles espoused by any one ideology or school of design.

The frustrations accompanying the bureaucracy-ridden assignments for INA Casa were worked out in Sottsass's personal concentration on 'the fragile scenery of the private domain'. In his designs for interiors, furniture, ceramics and lighting of this period, the Bauhaus's fascination with materials was combined with

Santa Maria Novella railway station in Florence, 1934. The building was the subject of a competition, won by a group led by Giovanni Michelucci. With its covered arrival corridor and continuous external glass panelling, the station is one of the best examples of inter-war Italian architecture.

55

a manipulation of shapes, reminiscent of work by Surrealist sculptors like Naum Gabo and Alexander Calder whom Sottsass also admired. The furniture that he exhibited at the Milan Triennale of 1947 displays the same sensuous, organic contours as that of Carlo Mollino, acclaimed as one of Italy's most gifted and original designers; plywood and metal tables, chairs and wall cabinets were moulded into curved surfaces to which geometric or organic functional and decorative detailing was applied.

This Triennale, the Eighth, was devoted to the problem of reconstruction and the housing and domes-

Construction, 1945: this sculpture shows the influence of artists such as Naum Gabo and Alexander Calder.

tic needs of lower-income groups. One section of it, the QT8 (Eighth Triennale Quarter) was a neighbourhood housing project in Milan for which Sottsass produced an (unexecuted) design for a local church in the same Rationalist style as the surrounding buildings. An emphasis on socio-economic needs was also evident within the exhibition halls; it was all part of the attempt to deal with the problem expressed by Ernesto Rogers in his first *Domus* editorial in 1946 as 'one of forging a taste, a technique, a morality as different manifestations of the same problem: the problem of building a society'.

The application of designers' talents to everything 'from a spoon to a city', as Tomas Maldonado later put it – the assumption being that the tasks and their solutions were essentially similar except for differences of scale – was seen as crucial to any national programme of planned regeneration. Industrial design acquired a new status, separate from architecture, because of its apparent connection with the Italian industries that were modernizing with government aid and making possible the production of cheap furniture and goods for the masses. In fact, this modernization programme was closer to myth than reality; fundamental inequalities of national life, like the north-south economic divide, remained and there was no national programme for converting wartime into peacetime production. As Sottsass puts it, 'For most of the people,the end of the war and the fall of the Fascist utopia were not exactly meaning vast open windows on a new future but just that Italy was going back to its traditional state...it would go on with the old social structures, with the old needs and solutions, the old rhythms tuned on agricultural economy and on a peasant culture with the Catholic religion at its head.'

Although he took part also in the Triennales of 1951 and 1954 and, like other designers, participated vigorously in the debates about design which were 'again a debate on society, a debate on life', although he was 'writing furious articles about the socially dangerous nostalgia for handicraft as a metaphor for conservatism', Sottsass seems always to have been scepti-

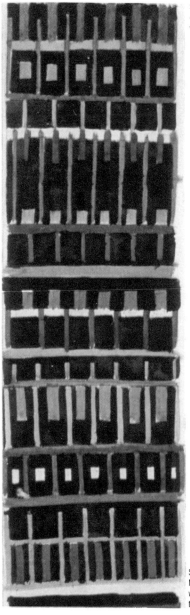

Sottsass's 1941 design for a carpet, left, recalls the textile designs of local craftsmen in Montenegro, where he spent most of the war years.

Sketch for a book cover, 1940, above, showing the influence of Mondrian. When Sottsass returned to Turin after the war, there was little architectural work available and 'fine art' activities like this occupied much of his time.

cal about the new vision of society based on industrial development as the source of new social energies. As he rightly points out, most Italian designers are architects who have had no special training in industrial technologies. This, he believes, means that 'fundamentally they are not trained to think of themselves as professionals at the service of industry or...as professionals dedicated to the improvement of the industry business.' It is certainly true that in post-war Italy contact between design and industry was infrequent and marginal.

There were exceptions to this pattern, notably at Olivetti where Marcello Nizzoli, designer of the Lettera 22 and Lexicon 80 typewriters, had been fully involved in the production process as a co-worker rather than an embellisher brought in at a late stage to 'style' the company's products. But Adriano Olivetti, with his progressive and humanistic approach to industrial organisation was unique in Italian industry and even Nizzoli was originally an artist, trained at the School of Fine Arts in Parma. For Olivetti, this broad cultural background had great advantages; originally brought in to work in the company's advertising office, Nizzoli produced many of their outstanding poster designs and the sculptural elegance of his products is enhanced with carefully applied graphics. But the fortuitous combination of artistic and industrial cultures was not always so happily fruitful.

Much has been made of the 'traditional' co-operation between industry and design in modern Italy but until the late fifties this was still very limited and existed mainly on a promotional level, for publicity purposes. Nizzoli's typewriters achieved an unprecedented and harmonious relationship between mechanism and body, now perceived as the great strength of Olivetti equipment, because of his direct, hands-on training and experience; younger designers were seldom able or willing to reproduce this 'manual' involvement. Mostly, they were architects who simply applied their architectural ideology and methodology to the design of objects. On a positive level, this sometimes led to the adoption of more advanced industrial and technologi-

Sculpture, 1946. Sottsass moved to Milan in 1946 and organized an international exhibition of modern art with Bruno Munari. His own work, in metal, was beginning to show the influence of the Constructivists.

cal procedures since the new young professionals were anxious to catch up with other industrial countries. In a *Domus* article on Charles Eames in 1947, for example, they had read of his plywood and steel furniture and the same year Vittoriano Vigano and Achille Castiglioni produced a plywood armchair that used new techniques of bending the material and applying it to the structure. Many young designers were embarrassed by manufacturing's dependence on manual, craftsmanlike execution; ironically,this has come to seem a great strength of Italian design and a basis for its international prestige. Observers from elsewhere are fond of citing intuitive mechanical understanding (which supposedly compensated for Italian soldiers' alleged military inadequacies and rendered them invaluable tank mechanics for the Allies) as a national characteristic that can salvage any situation from fixing clapped-out Lambrettas to developing state-of-the-art computers. Some credence can be attached to this but it also contains a fallacious view of the circumstances of Italian design's rise to prominence.

'Design arrived in Italy as theoretical thought, not as practice,' asserts Sottsass. He does not deny or underestimate the craftsmanship tradition but points out that the *culture* of design was imported into post-war Italy from outside. 'Design started as a political debate,' he argues. 'It provided an argument on which to hang theoretical discussions and inevitably took on a political colour.' As far as practical manifestations were concerned, very few examples of experimental design had been produced since the Fascists came to power two decades before. Apart from the typewriters that came out of Nizzoli's collaboration with Olivetti, begun in 1936, few designers had come near to producing any objects as remarkable as Livid and Pier Giacomo Castiglione's Phonola plastic radio receiver, developed with L. Caccia Dominioni in 1938 and described by Sottsass as 'very strange and surrealistic'.

While industrial reconstruction progressed, assisted by government aid and policies like the provision of cheap credit and resources, home market protectionism and low wage levels (made possible by the pool of immigrant labour from the South), designers were also

At the 1946 exhibition, Sottsass showed a series of delicate wood constructions suspended in air, reminiscent of Alexander Calder's mobiles.

doing everything they could to build the vision of a new, democratic future. Infected by a general optimism which flourished in spite of immense hardship and widespread unemployment, Sottsass remembers how 'Almost without money, almost without houses, with no factories and maybe no pencils and no brushes, everyone was thinking that they had to participate in designing the future of Italy, even the designers.'

The post-war Reconstruction programme gave Sottsass his first opportunity to participate in architectural building programmes. His schemes at Meina in 1951, left, and Arborea in 1953, below, were part of a series of government subsidized low-cost housing projects.

This welded sheet metal sculpture of 1947 recalls the work of Surrealist artists like Jean Arp who influenced Sottsass's fine art activities.

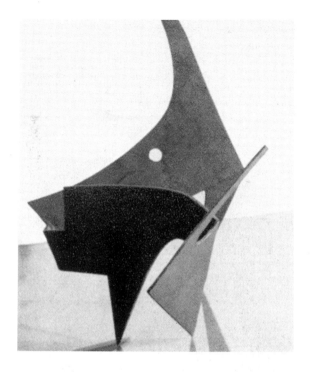

As well as writing articles 'about the special new beauty that may come out from the coolness, the anonymity and acidity of machine production', lecturing and exhibiting, designers were making a prolific contribution to the country's potential ranges of manufactured goods. According to Sottsass, they were designing 'an enormous quantity of chairs and armchairs and even a larger quantity of lamps and chairs again and lamps again that were all supposed to be super mass-produced and distributed all over the country for rich and poor people, all of them very beautifully designed to fit the vision of a new way of life.' This new way of life gave precedence to the welfare of the masses, to the satisfaction of their needs and the enrichment of their lives by industrial production and the designs themselves were often both beautiful and functional. They included projects by many of the individuals who are now legendary names in the story

63

Sottsass's product designs of the mid to late 1950s were highly sculptural. The table lamp, above, and wire flower-holder, left, were functional objects developed by moulding simple materials into abstract shapes.

of Italian design: Albini, the Castiglioni brothers, Gio Ponti, Belgiojoso. But most of this mass of pioneering, prophetic work was produced in such small quantities, if at all, that it barely saw the light of day.

'They never reached the masses,' says Sottsass. 'They never reached the poor because of the money; neither did they reach the real wealthy and conservative people, obsessed by antiques, by craftsmanship and finesse as status symbol. They may have reached some intellectuals, some crazy collectors, some barber in Sicily or some bartender in Calabria, fanatics of modernism. But mostly they reached a few exhibitions and a few magazines where they were published.' The reason for this is not, as he has heard 'some nervous British critics' suggest, that post-war Italian design was just made to be photographed and published in magazines because 'only Italians do such things...they have always been kind of smugglers anyway'. Nor is it because 'Italians always badly need advertisement...that's true also for companies that have just gone on the market like Italian designers' – the most silly reason, he thinks, for publishing work in magazines. It is because of the peculiar characteristics of Italian design and Italian industry in this post-war period.

Partly because most of the designers were architects, as much concerned with a social vision as with technical production, but mostly because they were Italian, accustomed to considering life as a performance,their designs represented more than physical objects. When they produced a sketch for a product or a piece of furniture they were also making a statement, transmitting a social and intellectual idea. Sottsass explains the special problem that this approach to design can entail:

> 'If the goal of your design is going beyond the
> physical presence of the product; if it is supposed
> to broadcast a much wider message and if –
> total disaster – there is nobody around produc-
> ing or distributing your design, which means
> that nobody is communicating to anyone your
> nice and beloved message, what do you do then?'

The answer, of course, is that 'you try to publish it in some magazine'. The result of this tendency is that there are now twenty or so design-related magazines published in Milan each month, many of them continuing the tradition, started in the twenties and thirties by *Casabella* and *Domus*, of using the publications as a place to discuss ideas as well as to present new designs. Sottsass himself has often been accused of using the media, the magazines, to gain maximum coverage for his ideas. He does not bother to point out that most of this publicity is the result of zealous pursuit by the many journalists who constantly bombard his studio

for copy. He simply accepts that he, possibly even more than other Italian designers, is designing 'provisory, metaphoric, allusive stages' for the drama of life. Given their purpose, which is simply to explain the play, it does not make much difference what form they are encountered in.

Unlike many of his contemporaries, Sottsass has never expended much time and energy in looking for industrial companies that will produce and distribute his 'fragile statements'. He has always worked 'only for friends'; even when he was designing products for industrial mass-production, he did so only in association with Roberto Olivetti and his uniquely enlightened company or he responded to personal requests to produce designs for sympathetic family companies like Alessi. Leaving aside the obvious factor of their exceptional levels of aesthetic quality and interest, Sottsass's designs have nevertheless received, without benefit of corporate or personal advertising and P.R. back-up, intense and wide-ranging media coverage. This is partly because of his character, his attractiveness and interest as a personality and his social situation as a cherished

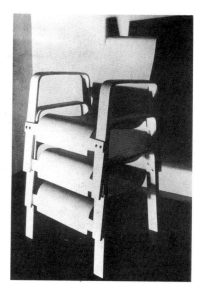

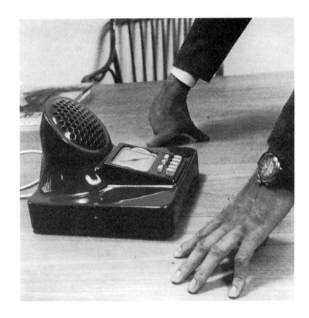

The plastic radio receiver designed by Luigi Caccia Dominioni with Livio and Pier Giacomo Castiglioni for the Phonola company in 1938 had a seamless moulded Bakelite shell. Shaped like a telephone, it could be hung from a wall or placed on a table. Sottsass described it as 'very strange and surrealistic'.

and generous participant within Milanese, and indeed international, creative and intellectual circles. His place within such circles has been further assured by his wife or 'companion' always having been a woman who was part of these groups in her own right. This was strikingly true of his first wife, Fernanda (Nanda) Pivano whom he married in 1949.

A writer and critic, Nanda Pivano achieved prominence in Italian literary circles as the translator of the American 'Beat Generation' poets and composers such as Ginsberg and Bob Dylan when she and Sottsass went to the USA a few years later she introduced him to these and other artists. Like the other women he has lived with, Pivano is an intellectual, profoundly involved with her own work. 'All my lovers, long or short-term, have had their own dignity, passions and creativity,' says Sottsass. He accepts totally the freedom and rights that the women's liberation movement has demanded and struggled for. 'I don't even think in terms of "she's a woman and I'm a man",' he says, but admits to displaying ambiguous attitudes towards feminism in his personal life.

'Culture conditions us, makes a man behave like a man,' Sottsass believes. His own mother probably did not expect her only son to share with the cooking and he admits that he automatically leaves that to his female companion, along with changing the sheets and reminding him that it is time for him to buy a new suit or attend an appointment with his doctor. 'It takes a hundred years to get over practicalities like these,' he thinks, though he has no problem in sharing everything to do with his intellectual and professional life with his partner. 'It is very beautiful living with someone with whom you discuss everything about your life and work,' he says, 'but that is not something you can bring about with laws or rules about how men and women should behave.'

Franco Albini was an important contributor to post-war experiments in contemporary furniture design. His malacca and bamboo cane 'Margherita' armchair, manufactured by Bonacina in 1950, proposed a new form while seeking to renew the Italian handicraft culture in its use of traditional materials.

In retrospect, it seems almost inevitable that Sottsass should have gone to the USA at some stage in the early 1950s, not only because the States were a powerful economic and cultural influence on Italy at that time but because he was an early believer in the idea that 'this planet will fare better if the inhabitants get to know each other better'. By the end of the war, he could already speak some English and German and he later picked up French from travelling and meeting people who spoke that language. 'I became a user of airplanes,' he says. 'In my travels I felt the globe was shrinking and each time it appeared smaller; that is good.'

When Sottsass speaks of internationalism, he does not mean the concerted action of the military alliances and bankers who, he believes, control most parts of the world and who will react immediately whenever they see something which is 'liable to interfere with the sale of their guns and their planes.' Nor does he have any illusions about 'the ancient ingrained reflex of groups of people ...to organise for defence'; but he despises 'provincial utopias'. 'I know that every man has his memories,' he has said. 'I, for instance, am a *ladino* (a peasant from the mountain villages)...I am what I am, I was born and lived as I lived. I will not obscure these facts but I also see no reason to sanctify them, to turn them into the exclusive aim of my life. Other people too have lived in particular circumstances with particular values but there is absolutely no reason to immure ourselves in defensive fortresses in which to play ad nauseam the scratchy record of our singularity.'

The incentive for working within an international context, as far as Sottsass is concerned, is 'the liberation of man, rather than the creation of a new international personality'. In the early fifties, the USA seemed alluringly free of 'European anxiety'; it offered a liberation from Italian preoccupations with national culture. This situation is quite different now, he thinks. In the last ten years, he suggests, Americans have developed a high level of nationalistic awareness, possibly because they feel weaker and less rich in ideas than before. The construction of a nationalistic vision

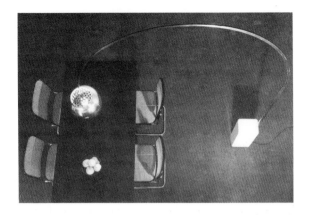

saddens him because he believes that a planetarian civilisation should be replacing national cultures.

'We have to work to develop an attitude that will permit different tribes to live together under the general umbrella of the planet,' he says. 'A tribe cannot close in on itself; instead of comparing ourselves with others or acting as missionaries to others, we should be developing communications with others.' He expresses the hope that the USA will not 'close up' to drastically, that it will open out again, because it is such an important entity. 'The USA,' claims Sottsass, 'practically invented our lives today.'

The 'massification', as he calls it, of industry, aviation, photography, telecommunications was indeed brought about by American initiatives, if not inventions. 'You can't fly with Icarus or Leonardo,' adds this frequent user of American aeroplanes. In the 1950s, when he went to live and work for a time in the USA, this Italian view of America as the source of developments that would create and sustain the new, global post-war society was a great deal more prevalent than now. The glimpses of American culture provided by the US military and naval presence in Italy at the end of the war widened as reconstruction and emigration exposed large sections of the Italian population to American products, attitudes and ways of life. What was revealed seemed to them a covetable model of economic prosperity and material comfort; now that they had finally emerged from war and internecine political conflicts, they began to demand some of this security and affluence for themselves.

Economic recovery, though it could not exactly be termed a 'boom' until the later 1950s, created aspirations for both services and consumer goods. Along with the chewing gum and Coca-Cola habits introduced by the American troops, Italians enthusiastically embraced the image of the comfortable, mechanised American home as portrayed in advertising and on television. This vision, epitomised by the cereal packet dream home kitchen, stuffed with electrical gadgets and dominated by the huge 'ice-box' purring in the corner, was not to become reality for any but a small minority of the population until considerably later. In the late forties and early fifties, the industrial production of modern consumer goods was still erratic and few truly innovatory objects were made in sufficiently high quantities at sufficiently low prices to reach the mass market.

The exceptions to this general situation include these objects which have now acquired iconic status; they are universally upheld as somehow epitomising the Italian talent for intuitive technical innovation combined with a native flair for endowing everything with visual style. The most fabled item in this legendary catalogue is the Vespa motor-scooter, designed by Corradino D'Ascanio in 1946.

Co-star (with actors like Audrey Hepburn, Sophia Loren and Marcello Mastroianni) of several movies in the 1950s heyday of Italian cinema, the Vespa characterized the Italian urban scene for foreign visitors and design-conscious observers. Ideally suited to negotiating the hills, bends and cobbled streets of typical Italian towns, it was economical to run and maintain, thus answering the need for cheap and functional motorized transport for workers, young people and the other groups who represented a growing demand for increased social mobility in post-war Italy.

The Vespa, manufactured by Piaggio, was quickly followed by the Lambretta, launched by Innocenti in 1947. The Pavoni coffee machine designed by Gio

Gio Ponti, who had founded *Domus* in 1928, was highly influential in the fields of architectural, product and furniture design. His 'Superleggera' chair, manufactured by Cassina in 1956, was based on a traditional form produced by local craftsmen in the fishing villages of Chiavari.

Ponti appeared the same year and together with Nizzoli's Olivetti typewriters and Battista Pininfarina's streamlined but compact Cisitalia car, also introduced in 1947, these 'classics' established Italian industrial design's reputation for functional Such brilliant innovations certainly deserved the admiration they aroused for their combination of style and utility but they were not entirely typical of the designs and products developed in Italy in the immediate post-war years.

Though he was responsible for the Pavoni machine, an emblem of the new Italian style, Gio Ponti was also the leading representative of contemporary attempts to mediate between the adoption of a modern, mass-production approach and the retention of artisan workshops applying manual skills to individual objects. His *Superleggera* chair, with its simple wooden frame and caned seat, was inspired by a traditional design made by the craftsmen of Chiavari, a fishing village near Genoa. But Cassina began to manufacture it in volume in 1956, using the new equipment that enabled them to become a leading producer of modern furniture for an international clientele. Cassina was one of the companies, based in Milanese suburbs like Meda, that had grown from small, family-run furniture workshops specializing in particular items. After the war, with the aid of grants, they modernized their production facilities and formed liaisons with architect-designers like Ponti to create goods that would appeal to a style-conscious, middle class market in Italy and beyond.

Ponti resumed his editorship of *Domus*, which he had founded 20 years earlier, in 1947. Under his direction, the magazine's former left-wing, Rationalist slant was modified; it began to advocate greater expressiveness in design, emphasizing its relationship to an Italian visual tradition rather than to modernist architecture. Its emphasis on what Ponti called 'the good life', which he equated with 'the level of taste and thought expressed by our homes and manner of living', also reflected current ideological and social aspirations, largely based on American models.

With his opposition to 'the supporters of handicraft as symbol of a lost golden age, to be recuperated the sooner the better...the place for the only real, respectable, institutional culture (which is the bourgeois one)', Sottsass's attitude to this new, more conservative tendency was ambivalent. In spite of his participation in the Triennales of the early fifties, he remained outside the industry-designer collaborations, continuing to work prolifically though mainly on an experimental level. But with the increasing demand for 'Italian style' design in America, even he was to be pulled into the two-way cultural currents – and one-way population movement – flowing between Italy and the USA.

While the streamlined curves enfolding the mechan-

Ettore Sottsass in 1949. He remembers how at that time, in spite of widespread poverty and unemployment, 'everyone was thinking that they had to participate in designing the future of Italy, even the designers'.

isms of Olivetti typewriters and Fiat cars were virtually imported from American automobile plants, there was an eager market in the US for the sculptural forms that dominated the 1954 Triennale. Organic shapes dominated both the decorative arts and industrial products sections of this show, where American observers may have noted Sottsass's asymmetrical ceramics, such as the tableware he had designed with Bepi Fiori in 1954. The *Italy at Work* exhibition of Italian craft and industrial products which toured the States in the early fifties might also have contributed to a growing demand for Italian-designed goods.

In any case, one progressive American company, Raymor of New York, decided that Sottsass should be the artist to create a new range of aluminium vases for them in 1955. These were actually manufactured in Italy, by Rinnovel, but the commission required Sottsass to make his first trip across the Atlantic to meet his patrons. The American industrial designer, George Nelson, had also worked for Raymor and Sottsass prolonged his stay to spend several months working in Nelson's New York office.

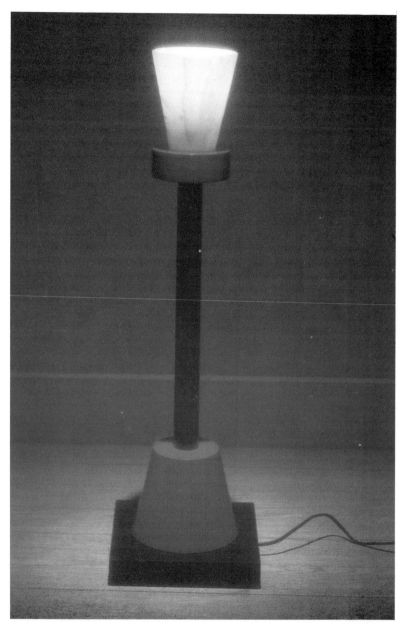

meditations on america and india

George Nelson, ten years older than Sottsass, was an architecture graduate of Yale University. The winner of a Prix de Rome in 1931, he spent the next two years travelling in Europe and was one of the first Americans to study the revolutionary new buildings of the European modern movement. He secured Mies van der Rohe an introduction to the USA and when he returned to the States in 1933, he founded *Architectural Forum*, a magazine which helped to promote modernist design. From 1936-46, he worked on various architecture and interior design projects, including the 'storage wall' office furnishing system which made his early reputation as a furniture designer.

Nelson worked for the Herman Miller organisation from 1946-47 and introduced Charles Eames to this company who later manufactured all Eames' designs. Though he had set up his own office in New York in 1947, Nelson designed the immensely successful 'Action Office' for Herman Miller in 1965; this was an early attempt to create a rational, humanistic office environment before computers took over many of the functions of manual equipment. Sottsass's office systems for Olivetti were a later version of the 'people-centred' office and the two men shared a distaste for commercial design with no theoretical or philosophical basis.

Nelson is closely associated with the design philosophy and educational programmes of New York's Museum of Modern Art and is probably better known for his work on committees, his writing and

Lamp in alabaster, granite, metal and lacquered wood from the 1985 Bharata collection, made by Indian craftsmen.

Designs for hangings, 1956: the same motifs were used by Sottsass on a poster for the 11th Triennale the following year.

his contributions to international conferences than for his actual designs. His ideological approach bound him more closely to European designers like Sottsass than to Americans like Raymond Loewy and other 'stylists'. But Sottsass, working in Nelson's office, came to understand and appreciate aspects of American culture that were never recognised by other Italian designers less sympathetic to US attitudes.

The USA had acquired its artistic heritage, and many of its artists, from Europe, he discovered, but this cultural background was dramatically modified by being 'filtered through America's own civilisation'. Sottsass enthusiastically embraced all aspects of this new world culture, observing the graphic language of commercial advertising with as much appreciation as he viewed the work of his favourite abstract expressionist artists like Willem de Kooning, Arshile Gorky and Jackson Pollock. His apparently effortless ability to recognize and absorb the qualities of both fine art and the imagery of popular culture and apply them to his own work has always been a great strength of Sottsass's designs. Years later, Memphis was to epitomize this tendency of combining 'high' and 'low' art with immense success.

Excited though he was by New York life, Sottsass never seriously considered remaining there permanently and he returned to Milan in 1957 in time to make a significant contribution to the Eleventh Triennale. Coinciding with Italy's entry into the EEC, that year's exhibition was devoted to the theme of 'Europe'. It jointly emphasized the Italian manufacturing industry's ability to produce goods that could compete

Nelson's 'Storage Wall' for the Herman Miller company, 1946. Like Sottsass's later work for Olivetti, it combined humanistic design with the rational application of functional principles.

successfully in European markets and the creative, artistic strength that gave these products their distinctive Italian qualities.

The room of Italian glass, designed by Sottsass, expressed both these strands; the objects themselves, testimony to a wealth of talent and skill, were displayed in an elegant, geometric grid of wooden surfaces, reminiscent of Mackintosh or Viennese art nouveau designs. For Sottsass, this rectilinear motif was quite a departure from earlier work though it recalls other typically Italian forms, such as the grilles and ceramic screen on his own low-cost housing or Carlo Scarpa's latticed structures. The geometric approach was incorporated into Sottsass's rich vocabulary of forms and still surfaces alongside other, more abstract patterning.

By stressing the important role of individual artist-designers, the Triennale of 1957 and subsequent years was promoting Italian industry, within an international context, as uniquely capable of devising innovatory forms for new consumer goods. This potential, they were implying, was a result of the country's exceptional

Jackson Pollock's 'Abstract painting'; Sottsass's unhesitating appreciation of the work of the abstract expressionists, Pollock especially, inevitably had repercussions in his own work, alongside the various other cultural influences he instinctively absorbs.

design strength. Sottsass describes how the old craftsmen, who first changed their small *botteghe* into mechanised workshops and then became 'real' industrialists – like Cassina and other furniture manufacturers – 'learned very fast that an industry, to be really complete with all the necessary technologies, has also to possess and use design. They also learned, obsessed as they had been for years by the designers' sauciness and aggression, that Italy had a lot of designers just ready to work for them.'

'They started to be more or less convinced that all those fucking prototypes published in magazines, all those drawings and those nonsense exhibitions, all those incomprehensible lectures, all that shouting about the future of life, about the future of society, might not be as crazy as they thought...The new industrialists learned instead that all that fussing around, all that turbulence could be...sold.'

'That was a great enlightenment, a great moment,' says Sottsass – with a certain amount of irony. He is referring to a period when industrial reconstruction and expansion and steady economic growth were bringing about huge increases in productivity; collaborations of designers and industry were effecting a transformation of Italy's physical and social environment. By the time

The Room of Italian Glass, designed for the Eleventh Milan Triennale in 1957. The geometric grid, reminiscent of Mackintosh and Viennese art nouveau, was a new development in Sottsass's work.

Sottsass returned to Italy in the late fifties, the 'boom' had begun to reverberate. Italian industry, with its cheap labour supply, new factories, new methods and new forms devised by designers, had begun to satisfy the collective wish for prosperity and security, the vision of American-style affluence and comfort that now became attainable for some, though by no means all, of the population.

Alongside developments in mass communications and the media, particularly television, design helped to repaint the picture of Italian domestic and social life. Many Italian women gained a new freedom and independence with the mobility offered by economical motor cars like Dante Giacosa's Fiat 500, the ubiquitous 'Cinquecento'. In their kitchens and living rooms, the copper pots and bulky wooden furniture handed down through generations were replaced by utensils and furnishings whose design had been born with them and whose forms owed more to new technology than to existing models.

Kartell's plastic kitchen accessories, Zanussi fridges and cookers, Candy washing machines, Brionvega televisions were elements of a total image that symbolized a new existence for the Italian working class. In their new motor cars, 90% of which were produced by Fiat by the beginning of the sixties, Milanese workers could drive to the lakes or mountains for the weekend. Their counterparts in southern Italy, and relatives who had not emigrated to work in the new factories of the north, had to wait longer for the products of affluence. In 1963, the *Autostrada del Sole* was constructed, enabling the stream of consumer durables to flow down to new markets in that other, poorer Italy. In the summer it was accompanied by convoys of tourists off to spend their new-found wealth and leisure in the sunshine, the only thing the south had more of.

Sottsass was not alone in feeling ambivalent about design's more active and central role in Italian social and economic life. A number of leading architects had refused to participate in the eleventh Triennale, arguing that it presented design principally as the domain of capitalist power and was narrowly preoccupied with design itself as an isolated phenomenon. The so-called *Casabella* group declared that 'the myth of the object as a secondary phenomenon of the fetishism of goods is a true characteristic of our times'. They were among the first observers to question the indiscriminate generation of goods whose appearance conveyed nothing about their technological, social or historical context.

Attempts to design greater expressiveness into objects included furniture by the architect, Vittorio Gregotti, whose 1956 chair for Azucena recalled Italian fin-de-siecle culture, and by the Castiglione brothers, whose 'San Luca' armchair for Gavina in 1960 was a quotation that used memory as a design material. Slightly later, Sottsass was to become the prime mover in an effort to establish relationships between objects and the human environment but it was the new status of design, and designers, as sales generators that enabled him to 'start working' at the end of the 1950s.

Individual designers were already beginning to be

The Zanussi cooker designed by Gino Valle in 1958 displays the clean lines and unfussy detailing that typified Italian consumer appliances of this period. This neat styling, combined with low prices, created a huge export demand for such goods.

The Candy washing machine, designed by Piero Geranzani for Eden Fumagalli, gained the 1960 Compasso d'Oro, the major award for Italian design that had been established by the department store, La Rinascente in 1958.

identified and promoted by manufacturing companies as valuable selling propositions. Their names seemed to carry some guarantee of the artistic quality that was considered an essential part of Italian design and to distinguish particular versions of mass-produced objects. The Castiglionis' work for Zanotta, Carlo Scarpa's furniture for Gavina and Marco Zanuso's for Pirelli's Arflex company are outstanding examples of the valuable results of industrial patronage. Another is Sottsass's early work for Olivetti, who first approached him in 1958.

Adriano Olivetti, the visionary and humane founder of the company, had certainly seen Sottsass's designs

Colourful plastic utensils by Kartell, like the thermos beakers designed by Gino Columbini in 1953, transformed the appearance of kitchens throughout Europe in the 1950s and 60s (above). Brionvega were prominent among Italian manufacturing companies who acted as patrons of contemporary design in the 1960s. The 'Doney 14' transistorized television set (right) was designed by Marco Zanuso and Richard Sapper in 1962.

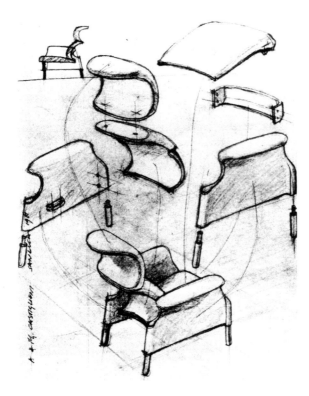

Pier Giacomo and Achille
Castiglioni's 'San Luca'
armchair for Gavina, 1961 was
a quotation that recalled the
'stile Liberty' thus
counteracting the disturbing
effect of radically new design.

for the various furniture companies he had now worked
for and possibly some ceramics and interiors done for
private Milanese clients. He called up and explained
that he would like Sottsass to head a team of designers
working within the company's new electronics section
but did not suggest that he should be put on the company's payroll of full-time staff. Instead, Olivetti was
offering him the kind of consultancy agreement that
most industrial designers only dream about.

Sottsass was to have complete 'cultural and practical
freedom' to work on personal commissions while
leading the group of designers – some based at Olivetti,
some in Sottsass's studio in Milan – who would be
working on Olivetti's very latest project, a system of

office computers. Such products were still regarded as rather futuristic at this time and few precedents existed for the packaging and styling of computer equipment destined for office environments. It is typical of Olivetti's far-sighted attitude that they approached this as a cultural, rather than just a technological, problem. Thus they appointed a chief designer whose experience in the area of technological products was minimal but who had demonstrated within the wide spectrum of his creative activity an exceptional concern with the social implications of design.

For Sottsass, the challenge seemed to incorporate his principal interests. Though working as an independent consultant outside the 'hierarchic-bureaucratic structures of industry', he would be involved in designing primary elements of the late twentieth century landscape of work. He has always felt that the maintenance of his independent status was important for himself and for Olivetti, since it gave him a position of strength in discussions with the company's engineers; but he

Marco Zanuso's 'Lady' armchair for Arflex proposed a softer shape for upholstered furniture by exploiting the flexible qualities of foam rubber.

also appreciated the opportunity to collaborate in this fascinating venture with such skilled enthusiasts as Olivetti's management and engineering teams and with their technical director, Mario Tchou, who became a close friend of Sottsass and had his apartment interior designed by him in 1963.

The first big Olivetti project Sottsass worked on was the ELEA 9003 computer system which consisted of a line of central processor cabinets each with two flanking cabinets that gave access to the card index. Sottsass immediately demonstrated his commitment to humanizing the office environment by lowering the cabinet heights to enable operators to see and communicate with each other. He also developed a network of connecting devices to facilitate the flexibility and growth of the system and he initiated an ergonomics research programme to help him devise a standard range of measurements that would relate ideally to the human scale.

The ELEA computer is reminiscent of Sottsass's later 'radical' furniture, not only in its visual monumentality but in its conceptual background. Unlike previous computers which were ranged along walls like cup-

In 1960, Sottsass designed an apartment interior for Mario Tchou, his close friend and associate at Olivetti. Tchou, an engineer and physicist, headed the company's electronic research laboratory where the Elea computer, designed by Sottsass, was produced. In November 1961, Tchou died in a car accident on the Turin-Milan motorway

boards, Sottsass's cabinets became a major, sculptural presence in the office environment and they could be arranged in different configurations to suit different interiors. Colour, a constant and active element in his work, played a major part in unifying their various parts and relating them to the whole environment. While the exterior of the cabinets was white with red detailing, the controls were daringly colour-coded in mauve, turquoise and yellow.

Though Sottsass was to continue a close and fruitful relationship with Olivetti as their leading consultant designer until well into the 1970s, many of his most

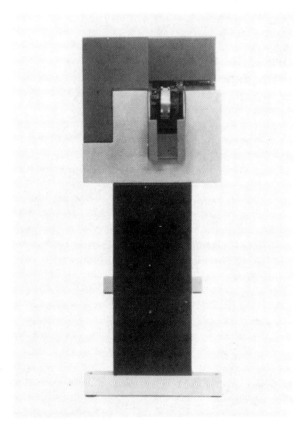

The 'ELEA 9003', Italy's first computer system. The cabinets represented a monumental presence in the office environment but operators could see over them to communicate with each other.

Sottsass's designs for Olivetti in the 1960s included innovative typewriters such as the Tekne 3 of 1964 (facing top). Its simple, definitive lines were intended to co-exist calmly with other office machinery. The Praxis 48 of 1964 (facing below) was widely adaptable, for use in any kind of office and elsewhere. The carriage and machine body formed a toy-like box shape from which the independent keyboard projects. The Logos 27 mechanical super-calculator of 1965 (right) was one of the most sophisticated pieces of technical equipment of its time and Sottsass's solid, sober form gave it a dignified character.

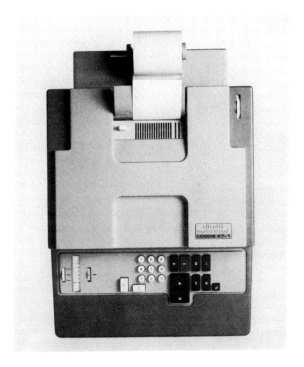

memorable and familiar consumer products were designed within his first few years with the company. His first electronic typewriter design, the Tekne 3 that he produced in 1960, reflected new techniques of cutting metal with its sharp lines that contrasted with more rounded precedents. Three years later, he presented the famous Praxis 48, an elegant and sophisticated typewriter, its shell a completely integrated form, the carriage flush with the machine body. *Domus* described this lightweight machine as 'a decorative object which can be left on the table' and it became one of the first status symbols in the office equipment category of cult objects.

By the mid-60s, Sottsass had added the Lettera De Luxe and Dora portable typewriters and ranges of electronic equipment such as the Logos 27 calculator to his Olivetti portfolio. Working as an independent, free-

lance designer from his own studio, he had also completed a number of interesting interior designs, furniture projects and ranges of ceramics. But it was partly thanks to his great friendship with Roberto Olivetti, who took over the management of the company when his father Adriano died in 1960, that he had been able to work at all; that he was, indeed, still alive.

In 1962, Sottsass fell critically ill, suffering from a rare kidney disease. His friend's generosity enabled him to travel to Palo Alto in California to be treated by one of the world's leading specialists in this area of medicine. By this man's skill and 'some miracle', says Sottsass, his life was saved. It, or at least his outlook on life, was also changed. Lying in a hospital bed for months, soon after a trip to India in 1961 which had also affected him profoundly, he thought long and seriously about his role as a designer, amongst other things.

Sottsass had always been interested in ancient cultures – Sumerian, Egyptian, central American – and since he was a child, had read more books on archaeology than any other single subject. He had an urge to see and know about people and places that 'have left traces in our memories, from magic to religion to fanaticism...technologies of life which are not always rational, like those of the East, which progress by constant training of the body and mind.' His 'nostalgia for disappeared lives' almost inevitably led him to India whose fundamental importance, for Sottsass, lay in its being a non-Catholic country.

'Catholicism is always dividing life into the material and the spiritual,' he explains, 'but to Indians there is no division; the spirit is coming from matter and matter takes its form from the spirit. That means that you can, you must, work on the material level.' In India, he found confirmation of what he had always suspected – that the world is perceived more through the senses than through the mind. And the senses, Indians believe, can be exercised and heightened, through yoga for instance, so that they can absorb more and react more sensitively.

Unlike Catholicism, Indian religions do not negate pleasure, 'the pleasure of sex, of food, the pleasure of pleasure.' It was very interesting to Sottsass to find that in India, 'pleasure can be the road to bliss'. It seemed to suggest an opening for those of us trapped in a world of materialism and to indicate that we could continue to build our materialistic civilisation 'without going into danger'; we might even be able to reach certain, more profound spiritual areas. Finding a way of doing this, with design being used as one of our means, is something that continues to absorb him.

The other contrast that Sottsass observed between Indian civilisation and our own concerned the speed with which we consume everything in the West. 'In the world of consumerism, everything has to be taken very fast because there is always something else to be taken after it; we are always running after *having* something. It would be very interesting to be able to stop this running and create a new awareness of what you have or may have.' The only way of achieving this, he thinks, is through some form of ritualism. Rituals do still exist in modern civilisation, he believes, but they are few and 'very concentrated'.

As an example of ritual in western society, Sottsass cites the (in Italy) Sunday afternoon football match. 'There you have this huge green pitch with the vast blue sky above and maybe 80,000 people taking part in this great ritual of watching a game, going home, tired, having dinner and falling asleep.' But we need smaller rituals, too, he believes, common procedures that we have lost because we have fallen out of the habit of observing them. 'Our relationship with objects, for example; today, objects are constantly being used, misused, re-used with no awareness of the object itself as an element of your life.' In India, Sottsass found, the situation was very different and 'this attention to materialism was very interesting to me.'

Without suggesting that the Indian way of life represents 'the maximum programme for society', Sottsass believes that westerners might benefit from adopt-

The Bharata collection of 1985 grew out of Sottsass's continuing fascination with India and its 'culture of objects'. With designs like these jugs in silver and brass, he was trying to reawaken an awareness of ritual in domestic life.

All the Bharata (the Sanskrit word for India) objects were made by Indian craftsmen using traditional skills. This end table is made in lacquered wood and inlay.

ing certain aspects of that way and integrating them into a new programme for their own lives. He admires the way that Indian people seem to know how to face poverty and death: 'Though they are very poor, they appear elegant, smiling, refined in their gestures and in the ceremonies that they carry out with one flower (not 1000). Through thousands of years of poverty, illnesses, love, death they have built up a net of filters so that disaster does not hit them directly. In the West, we tend to hide disaster. For example, I realized that in Milan I see perhaps one funeral a year; in Madras, I saw maybe two or three every day. But disaster is a friend with which we have to live.'

The greater awareness of objects that Sottsass refers to is based, he thinks, in Indian craftsmen's almost exclusive concentration on making religious objects; mostly, that is, instruments of ritual such as statues for temples. 'There has,' he says,' been a great religious programme for objects since ancient times.' Thus their makers and users are very conscious of what an object *is*, both functionally and symbolically.

The small number of possessions found in an ordinary Indian home also contributes to this greater consciousness of objects. 'An Indian family has nothing,' Sottsass explains. 'They sit on the floor, eat with their hands, their dresses are just a piece of fabric; so that a small bronze bowl, for instance, becomes something of immense importance in the environment. It becomes an instrument for thought, for meditation,

95

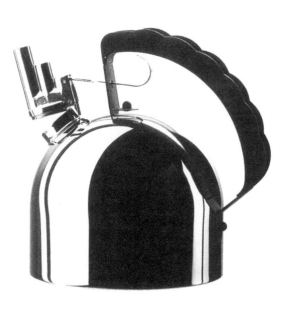

Alessi kitchenware includes
this kettle designed by Richard
Sapper

for signifying that someone is a leading person in
society. And because of this importance, craftsmen
work these objects more carefully, more subtly, so that
they become beautiful, vibrating with mystery and
magic.'

This culture of objects is something we do not have
at all in the West but Sottsass thinks that through design
we might try to recuperate the idea of the refined,
highly detailed object. The problem is that 'we have
thousands of objects...if you put a well-designed thing
in a window with hundreds of others, it means
nothing. So it is difficult, almost impossible to reach
that intensity – but it is something I am trying to do,
if I can, sometime. That is why I went through this
experience with Indian craftsmen.'

The experience he refers to is the creation of a group
of objects that he had made by Indian craftsmen in
1988. While preparing this *Bharata* (Sanskrit for India)
collection, he learned that 'you can reach a certain

intensity in designing an object. Not just in terms of detailing for the sake of industry or elegance or beauty but detailing to the point that the object becomes an instrument for a ritual of life. Sometimes an ancient Etruscan or Sumerian or Egyptian object can also have this intensity, this quality that makes you cry when you see them.'

Inevitably, Sottsass – whom many perceive principally as a designer of technological artifacts for Olivetti – is asked how these feelings about the role of objects can be reconciled with working for the mass production enterprises of industrial civilisation. 'I don't

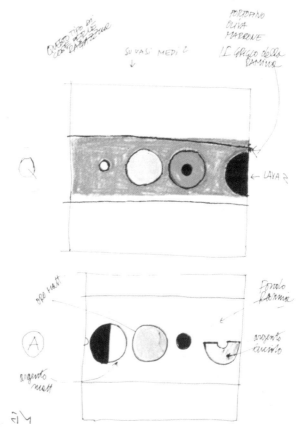

Sketches for 'Ceramics of Darkness' 1962-63. This collection of cylindrical pieces commemorates the long, dark days of Sottsass' near-fatal illness in the early sixties.

know if it's possible,' he replies, 'but I have noticed that there is now a general desire to have better food, for instance; not just in terms of health but more beautiful food that is put together on the table in a more beautiful way. Eating is, or was, a great ritual that was lost with the arrival of fast food habits but I don't think that they represent the maximum that we can expect from industrial society. The observation and the awareness that you are eating good food that is beautiful to look at is in some ways a cure, part of a recuperation. Dress too, is recuperating a certain intensity; it's not just a sense of design but a sense of ritual. The sexual ritual of the miniskirt, for example, is much more developed than it was 50 years ago. Even fast food in terms of environment, image and so on is moving forward, reaching perfection.'

In many other aspects of people's lives, in the home for example, Sottsass observes a desire to acquire, through design, a greater awareness of their individuality, of their own life and their own possibilities. He continues to design not for the sake of producing more

The Shiva ceramics of 1964 celebrated Sottsass's return to health and creative activity. Appropriately, the chief Hindu deity is associated with a dance incarnating the forces of creation, life and energy.

'Ceramics are older than the Bible and Jesus Christ, older than all the poems that have ever been written, older than goats and cats, older than houses, older than metals,' wrote Sottsass. In the late 1950s, his work in this medium included these enamelled plates decorated with symbolic shapes.

objects but to increase that awareness, to show people that objects do not represent reality but are a metaphor for something spiritual and beautiful. It is not necessary to possess them; in fact, to become free 'you must get rid of these beliefs that possession is something special'.

These are the kind of difficult, philosophical questions that Sottsass would stay up all night discussing with Roberto Olivetti. Their attitude to industrial production was similar to that of the creation of a work of art and clearly somewhat different from the usual approach to commercial manufacturing.

Things are rather different now, of course; Olivetti has been forced to become more competitive and Sottsass has been less involved with the company since the mid-1970s when he bequeathed his position to his former assistant, Michelle de Lucchi. But he emphasizes that the company is still exceptional in retaining a great sense of responsibility towards society. In this sense, it is similar to the firm of Alessi, for whom he has designed domestic utensils in metal and ceramics. 'Alessi really believes that industrial design is not just a way of selling things but that it has a responsibility to produce environmental changes. I can work with Alessi but I could not work with Fiat, for example.'

The trip to India preceding his illness, and contemplated upon at length while he convalesced, and the travels in west coast America meeting hippies, the Beat poets, Hell's Angels that he undertook with Nanda after his recovery profoundly influenced the work Sottsass was to produce in the early 1960s. First, he commemorated his dark days of suffering by producing, in 1963, a group of ceramics that was his earliest attempt at 'raising the object to a level of concentration so as to release it from its lesser functions and place it within a higher cultural sphere'. This was the 'Ceramics of Darkness' collection of 70 cylindrical pieces, sombrely coloured and decorated with circular symbols like the mandalas of mystic religions.

The following year, another collection of ceramics was dedicated to Shiva. The dance of the principal Hindu deity, incarnating the forces of creation, life and energy, was the ideal metaphor for Sottsass's celebration of his return to health and creative activity. These vases were described as 'spiritual diagrams', the outcome of using design 'as memorandum for the mental and psychic operations necessary for liberation'. They seem to symbolize not only his liberation from illness but also the social freedoms embraced by the hippies and the freedom from Western materialist ideology that he had found in India. With the Shiva vases, he was trying to arouse that Indian awareness of objects which related them to the rituals of life rather than just seeing them as functional products.

The abstract shapes decorating the Shiva vases seem to have been inspired by the iconography of Eastern religious art. Typically, Sottsass had absorbed into his work visual characteristics that expressed the cultural memories he had built up on his travels. Often they appear as decoration on the surface of fabrics, objects and ceramics. Some earlier enamel ware, for example, had displayed the blobs and stripes of the Abstract Expressionist painting he had admired in New York. A terracotta series for Raymor in 1957 had much simpler, traditional patterns reflecting the rustic origins of this vernacular Italian material. Later on, his discovery of American Pop Art was clearly celebrated in the forms and surfaces of items of furniture. The modes of expression Sottsass could employ to transmit his enthusiasms and experience were apparently endless.

His recovery from illness was celebrated not only in ceramics but in jewellery, painting and interior design. All his work of the early 1960s vibrates with colour and bold shapes and patterning. Eastern influences are prevalent, from the oriental partitioning in the Tchou

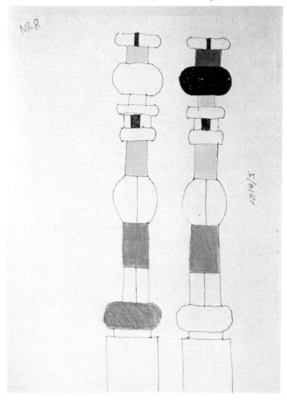

These sketches for ceramic objects from 1964 are characteristic of Sottsass's work of this period. Vibrant colour and bold shapes indicate an optimism about contemporary life.

apartment with its red and purple walls to the mandala-like imagery of his 1963-64 series of paintings. The paintings, however, with titles like 'Marilyn Monroe' (1963) also indicate his fascination with contemporary popular culture. His designs of the mid-1960s were almost bound to reflect the Pop Art movement that shared his own mood of optimism and rescued from oblivion the vibrant imagery of the consumer society.

Sottsass was aware that design had fallen behind in its attempt to lead the race to produce, to generate more and more products with greater and greater originality. It was all designers could now do, he realized, to keep up with other forms of visual culture, like fashion, through which young people especially were expressing a new sense of freedom and affluence. In 1964, he wrote, 'I looked about me, with my hair going grey, and the worst thing about it was not so much that my hair was grey, as that the young women had wrong-footed me with their aggressiveness; they had beaten me to the mark because what I wanted to do with furniture they had already done with their white canvas boots, with their multicoloured fancy stockings, decorated with stripes, coloured squares and dots.'

Only superficially deterred by the young women's hosiery, Sottsass proceeded to design a remarkable set of furniture that embodied the energy of Pop culture while confronting conventional opinions about consumption and the role of objects. The range of furniture produced for Poltronova in 1965-66 incorporated the graphic iconography and vivid colours of Pop painting and other contemporary art movements. The plastic laminate surfaces and traffic-light motifs denote a relationship with the wider environment of mass culture while the bright diagonal stripes and geometric shapes recall the 'edge' paintings and minimalist sculptures of American artists like Frank Stella and Sol LeWitt. But it was in their monumentality and powerful presence that these pieces signalled such a departure from orthodox furniture design.

Sottsass's desire to establish relationships between people and objects first became apparent with the ELEA computer system, an attempt to minimalist the

Sketches for jewels, ceramics and glazed plates, 1963. Referring to his work at this time, Sottsass wrote, 'I have tried as best I can to gather together the terms of a new vitality and, where and how I was able, to collect the shapes, colours and symbols that could represent the change in the images of this century.'

103

In addition to his strong influences from the East, the Pop Art movement excited Sottsass in the way it celebrated the imagery of the consumer society and its idols, like Marilyn Monroe (below). 'Homage to Honda', 1967, (top) is part of a series of furniture that borrows from the iconography and graphics of Pop Art. It thus relates more closely to mass culture than comparable 'designer furniture'

alienating character of the office environment. The Poltronova series, coming after his trip to India, also communicated a perception of objects in the home environment as instruments of ritual. These massive, monolithic pieces certainly looked the part of altars for the rituals of domestic life. They seemed to demand something from the consumer rather than just standing passively as status symbols, waiting to be replaced by the next fashionable design, the latest version to be consumed and discarded in its turn.

This furniture was clearly symbolic though of what, startled customers were probably uncertain. Of the ritual nature of keeping house, perhaps – the pieces had mystical names like Nirvana; of the ubiquitousness of commercial imagery; possibly of consumption itself – most of the items were wardrobes or cupboards for putting other things in. Whatever the specific references, Sottsass had produced furniture that expressed both function and meaning. His depiction of the relationships between the human and the material environment had gone beyond the merely stylistic and was moving towards more extreme manifestations.

new domestic landscapes

In 1960, the film-maker Federico Fellini made *La Dolce Vita*, an evocative, seductive, sceptical and moving account of a day and night in the life of chic, privileged Roman society. Some years later, Sottsass recalled 'the vision of a young, modern, optimistic, aggressive, excited, spreading middle class, ready to take possession of everything that could be offered by modern industrial culture; ready to destroy and to consume everything that would stand in their way or threatened their sunny, happy future'. Though he could easily, and accurately, have been describing the film, he was actually referring to the same social situation that Fellini had portrayed on celluloid. It was an image that typified contemporary life in Italy for many observers from elsewhere and was, in part, a true reflection of prosperous, middle class Italian existence.

For Sottsass, the second half of the sixties represented 'the big marriage between Italian designers and industry...music all over, information all over, fashion all over, art all over, TV all over, sports all over, hospitals all over, psychoanalysts all over, technology – Christ – all over and design, too – Christ – design, too, all over.' Clearly, he did not share the unreserved delight of many of his compatriots that Italian design had become a symbol of international affluence and chic. Rather, he saw this latest phenomenon as just another instance of design providing a backdrop for the current act in the drama of Italian life.

'Italian designers...knew very well how to contribute to shape the stage for that new immense event, for

Sottsass at his 1965 exhibition of giant ceramics in Milan. His most extreme statements about the mystical qualities of objects have always been made through the medium of clay.

107

the new consumerist society, he reflects. By the mid-60s, they had certainly developed exactly the right formula for meeting the demand, at home and abroad, for objects that reflected the streamlined, efficient, style-conscious lifestyle of modern young people with spending power. The designers' immense success in satisfying an international desire for such goods owes a great deal to the peculiar nature and structure of Italian industry.

Still able, in the early sixties at least, to rely on a huge pool of immigrant labour from the south and not under any great pressure from the country's weak trade unions to increase wages, manufacturers could also rely on a constant supply of cheap energy and materials from government-controlled producers. They were thus able to keep their prices well below those of foreign competitors who were anyway unable to match the talent and inventiveness of Italian designers. Italian style had surpassed Scandinavian style as the smart contemporary aesthetic and post-war reconstruction in Germany and Japan was not quite advanced enough to present a serious threat of rivalry in the area of technological design and production.

The Fiat X1/9 designed by Marcello Gandini at Bertone had a convertible roof that could be stored in the boot - perfect for the streamlined, efficient lifestyle of the new affluent Italian youth.

Pio Manzu's at Fiat proposed
this new city taxi in 1968,
prefiguring later concern about
urban traffic congestion.
Unfortunately, his prototype
was never developed (top).
Franco Albini, with Franca
Helg, designed the Milan
underground stations as an
integrated, subterranean
environment (below).

The *stile Italiana* of the sixties was, as Sottsass says,
'technologically oriented, so that it looked very
modern; it was simple, easy to understand, democratic,
not too expensive, functional, light; it was clean, as they
say, coloured, funny sometimes, it looked elegant sometimes, even rich sometimes, it looked even avant-garde.'
Numerous familiar examples could be used to illustrate
this definition: cars, buses, even Franco Albini's Milan
underground stations but above all, products for the
home. It was in the home that the consumer revolu-

tion was most noticeable and most advanced and its effects were seen in the living room, the bathroom and especially in the kitchen.

In the high blocks of flats that sprawled over the outskirts of northern cities like Milan and Turin, and in the spacious apartments carved out of palazzos in the centre and in other cities throughout Europe, kitchens were transformed by colourful plastic washing-up bowls, lemon squeezers and waste bins designed for Kartell by Gino Columbini and by sleek refrigerators and washing machines by Gino Valle for Zanussi. In more affluent homes, Kartell plastic stacking chairs by Joe Colombo, Vico Magistretti's moulded Selene chair for Artemide and his rush-seated 892 chair for Cassina might be placed beside Colombo's Spider lamp for O Luce or the Castiglionis' Arco lamp for Flos and their Mezzadro tractor seat chair for Zanotta. The picture of total stylishness would be completed with Enzo Mari's ceramics for Danese, Sergio Asti's glassware for Salviati, Brionvega televisions and the black box' radio by Mario Zanuso and Richard Sapper – and Ettore Sottsass's red plastic Valentine typewriter for Olivetti.

Sottsass is aware that a list of 'good' Italian designers of that period would have to include his own name but dismissing this as 'too boring', he prefers to concentrate on another side to this picture of contented consumerism. He was prematurely aware that all this comfort, all these possessions did not produce the ultimate satisfaction that might have been expected to accompany them. In some cases, this was clearly predictable; for the immigrant workers from southern Italy, a few electrical gadgets and a certain amount of

Bright plastic utensils, like these Kartell lemon squeezers of 1959, heralded a more colourful decade that exploited cheap new materials.

Plastic was applied for the first
time to the design of furniture.
Joe Colombo, in his tragically
short career, produced several
classic plastics like these
stacking chairs for Kartell
(above left). His 'Spider' lamp
for O Luce, designed in 1965,
was awarded the Compasso
d'Oro in 1967 and remains a
20th century design icon.
· Magistretti's 1963 '892' chair
for Cassina (above right) also
became an ubiquitous feature
in every design-conscious
home.

domestic privacy were inadequate compensation for being cooped up in high-rise buildings, isolated from the community life, kinder climate and outdoor, social existence of their native villages.

Ironically, the diet of spaghetti and tomatoes that was the staple of the poverty-stricken south was often reproduced in the affluent north; meat, unlike machinery, was not subsidized and was consequently expensive, often beyond the means of modestly paid factory workers churning out cars and consumer durables for the bourgeoisie. Eventually, in the late 1960s, dissatisfactions with such inequalities found a voice; stronger unions adopted the militant tactics demonstrated by the students in the protests of '68 and extracted better wages and conditions from manufacturers already under pressure from a credit squeeze.

Sottsass, in these years, was becoming less concerned with material needs than spiritual wants. 'So here we are,' he said of the mid-60s, 'with a landscape that looks very clean, beautiful and happy. Are we very satisfied?' The answer, he suspected, was "no" because 'consumerism has developed a new kind of culture called, if I am not wrong, materialistic culture. That means a culture that deals much more with the body than with the soul, much more with the realm of the senses than with the spirit. Consumerism has developed ...a culture that thinks that "the bliss" is only reachable through the total control and exercise of the rituals concerning the body.'

Achille and Pier Giacomo Castiglioni's 'Mezzadro' chair was designed for Zanotta in 1957. The painted metal tractor seat, resting on a steel support, is surprisingly comfortable.

Ceramics designed by Enzo Mari for Danese, like these reversible, high quality plastic vases of 1969, completed the domestic picture of total style in late sixties Italy.

The alliance between design and industry disturbed Sottsass because he thought it represented an evasion on the part of the designers, a reluctance to confront the real needs of people and the real role of design. In their desire to see their projects executed and their designs produced, they were, he believed, avoiding the reality of industrial culture. 'Sometimes Italian design of that period seemed to be looking for absolute beauty, for a sort of total pureness, for total abstraction; it seemed to be looking for an ideal aseptic area, where the shrewdness, the cynicism, the hardness, the mystifications, the intrigues of industry could be hidden or forgotten or maybe not even considered.'

In embracing industry and technology so wholeheartedly, designers, Sottsass asserted, were rejecting engagement with political and social problems, turning away from the forces that had shaped and given birth to Italian design. 'For many people, science and technology... industry also, seem to belong to that sheltered area where social struggles, social disasters, do not enter, do not appear, where the play of history can be avoided. Science and technology seem to have their own independent life, their own independent destiny; they seem to be continuously purified by their abstraction, by their nostalgia for the absolute, for the beauty of the absolute. And many designers, like many artists, thought that they could enter that sheltered area, that they could save and be saved, that they could be forgiven for their beautiful marriage with the not so very honest and not so pure bride that is industry.'

Whether or not as a result of closer collaboration with industry, much of the reforming idealism that had characterized Italian design of an earlier post-war period seemed to have evaporated by the mid-60s. In the previous two decades, designers had taken the initiative. Their aim was to develop innovatory objects whose forms and functions incarnated a new visual character for the post-war environment and symbolized a different way of life. Now they seemed content to play a more marginal role, limiting themselves to simply turning out sufficient products to enable industry to maintain its profit levels and keep pace with consumer demands.

The objects they produced were invariably elegant, attractive, opulent in a restrained and minimalist manner, and could be placed within the harmonious 'domestic landscape' of an affluent middle class home with no disruption to the general impression of

The black box aesthetic arrived in Italy in the early seventies, heralded by Zanuso and Sapper's 'Black 201' television for Brionvega, designed in 1969.

sophisticated good taste. These objects seemed to indicate an unquestioning acceptance of established patterns of production and consumption that disturbed Sottsass. His own involvement with industry, limited and unusually flexible though it was, had convinced him of the need to engage in constant debate about manufacturing's social responsibility and the effects of consumer capitalism. He was aware of the dangers of allowing industry to dominate and control the production of goods, partly because of the threat to its own survival.

Inevitably questioned about his own role in influencing patterns of consumption and use, Sottsass replied, 'It is true that, being designers, we serve industry and its interests...the designer can and should participate in well-focused political discussions with those who pay the piper and do everything in his power before submitting and becoming, in fact, a slave. Also, one can do much outside of industry...from time to time, industry should be reminded of the damage it causes... if industry will go on forcing the consumption level of society, it will have to develop faster and more flexible machinery to catch up with developments initiated by

115

Sottsass's 'Valentine' portable red typewriter of 1969 was, as he put it, 'invented for use any place except an office, so as not to remind anyone of monotonous working hours but rather to keep amateur poets company on quiet Sundays in the country or to provide a highly coloured object on a table in a studio apartment'. It quickly acquired cult status as a fashionable accessory.

itself. The consumer explosion, engineered by industry, might yet turn out to be a Frankenstein monster destroying its creator.'

Throughout the decade from the mid-1950s, design had been a major instrument of an economic and political policy directed towards the radical, even brutal, modernization of Italy. Designers collaborated readily, carried away by the post-war enthusiasm that Sottsass described as having its roots in the political optimism that surfaced after many years of Fascism. 'The novelty was in the fact that the Italians offered the world a new kind of home, more colourful, joyful, optimistic and with sense of humour... at long last we were free and the future was bright and promising. Only much later did it dawn on us that maybe reality operated by different rules.' When he observed, one of the first designers to do so, that industry was tending to relegate design to a propagandist, profit-maximizing role, he began to heed his own advice and 'do much outside industry'.

'Was it right to fill our homes with plastic objects? Did not industry exploit the consumer?' were the kind of questions Sottsass and a few other designers began to ask around 1965. By 1966 his work was starting to challenge and undermine contemporary notions of good taste as seen in the pages of *Casa Vogue, Abitare, Interni* and the other glossy magazines that had emerged to stimulate and support the designer/consumer network. His 'tower furniture' prototypes for Poltronova, for instance, were a far cry from the new but well-mannered and elegant pieces by Bellini or Magistretti.

There was no question of objects like these merging politely into the stylish, modern living room alongside designer classics like Tobia and Afra Scarpa's seating or the Castiglioni brothers' lighting. Instead of fitting in quietly like soothing status symbols, these massive pieces demanded attention; they seemed to compel some kind of user interaction, forcing the consumer out of a passive role to become an active participant in domestic rituals. This notion of consumption as a basic element in giving meaning to objects was to be a central idea of the 'Radical Design' movement of the

In the early sixties, Tobio and Afra Scarpa helped to invent a category of elite, luxurious modern furniture design with solid wood chairs upholstered in leather or expensive fabrics, like this model 917 for Cassina.

Sottsass's vision of the future, in which individuals would create their own surroundings to suit their way of life, was shared by radical architectural groups like Superstudio. Their 'Continuous Monument' series of 1969 provided a basic grid on which to develop these flexible environments (above). Archizoom were the other leading participants in the radical design movement of the late sixties. Pop and kitsch were quoted in contemporary objects cum sculptures like these 'Dream Beds' of 1967 (left).

late 60s and early 70s. Sottsass also prefigured another of the big themes of the decade by demonstrating a concern with the total physical environment.

He was closely associated with the radical groups that emerged primarily from the schools of architecture in Florence and Venice. Superstudio and Archizoom, the two most active, published and exhibited several projects, like 'Continuous Monument' and 'No-Stop

City' which envisaged a flexible environment that inhabitants would adapt to express and fulfill their own personality and functional requirements. Sottsass echoed this idea within the realm of objects with his giant ceramics of 1967. Like the architects' 'environments' these pieces did not impose specific patterns of use or relate to more orthodox forms of furniture. They stood like totems, challenging the consumer, provoking a response and encouraging the more ritual approach to objects that Sottsass had observed and admired in India.

The significance of the various groups of ceramics that Sottsass produced at this time depended on their impact as presences in the environment rather than their success as functional objects. They were his means of exploring and arousing the awareness of objects that he encountered in the East and, symbolically, they linked ancient and contemporary culture. The 1967 exhibition of 'Menhirs, Gas Pumps and Columns' in Milan, for example, was a collection of monoliths redolent of both antique civilizations and, with their boldly coloured surface decoration, popular modern imagery. His fascination with the ancient world combined, as it would constantly in the future, with his curiosity about the whole spectrum of contemporary visual culture.

The appeal of clay seemed to lie in its atavistic qualities; the reason he was using it, he said, for another exhibition of giant ceramics in Stockholm in 1969, 'must be because the first libraries were made with pieces of terracotta and the tower of Babel was also made with terracotta. Even the Colossus in the dream of Nebuchadnezzar had terracotta feet; the first failures of mankind had to do with terracotta.' His most extreme statements about the mystical qualities of objects are almost invariably made through the medium of ceramics. For instance, the 1969/70 'Tantra' and 'Yantra' series of flower vases were based, he explained, on geometrical compositions representing 'a particular force whose power or energy increases in proportion to the abstraction and precision of the diagram.'

But as always, it was the catholic (definitely with a

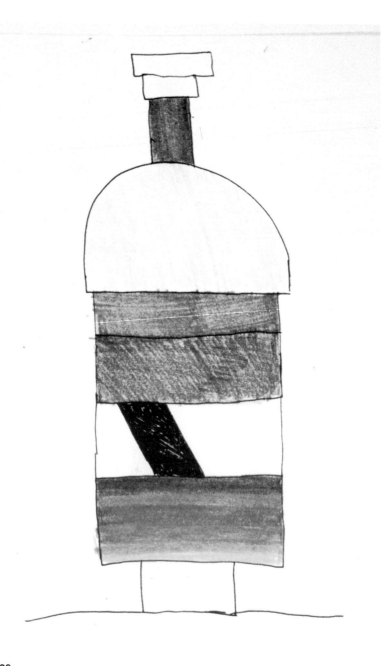

Drawings, left and right, for Sottsass's exhibition of large ceramics at the Galleria Sperone in Milan in 1967. 'Ceramics can bear anything,' Sottsass has written, 'sweet, old dry terracotta bears everything, cultures, so ethnologists tell us, societies, people, nations, kingdoms, sultanates and empires.'

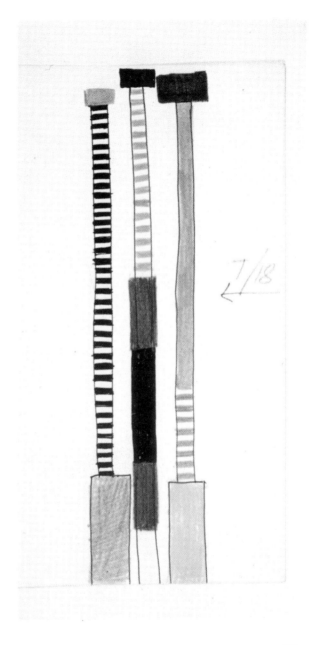

small 'c') nature of Sottsass's inspirations and vision that lent these pieces such impact. While incorporating the eternal qualities of mathematically created sculptural forms, they also reminded observers of Art Deco radios and the colour symbolism of their glazes was uncompromisingly modern; mauve, for example, was used as a 'super-vulgar colour, very much liked by old prostitutes'. Brash modernity and classical stillness combined, too, in the 'grey furniture' group of 1970 which deliberately confounded the commercial approach to selling furniture.

'Grey is a very sad colour, maybe the colour which my hairs are going into;...a colour that will create some problems for anyone who would like to use it for advertising detergents, toothpaste, vermouth, aperitifs in general, Coca-Cola, *elettro-domesti*, deodorants and all that.' It would also create problems for people who wanted modern designer furniture to provide a soothing background setting that was a constant and reassuring reminder of their affluence and good taste.

The huge neon-lit bed, mirror and cupboards, the pedestal table and chairs were all made out of shiny

'Grey Furniture' group of 1970 (above). Plastic forms and eerie neon lighting create a hermetic environment to encourage reflection on the power of objects, while isolated from the conventional consumer environment. The 'Tantra' and 'Yantra' ceramic flower vases of 1969-70 (right), inspired by Sottsass's reading about Tantric culture: 'Yantra', we read, 'is essentially a geometrical composition: but to understand its nature, one has to go beyond the notions of geometry into those of dynamics.'

grey plastic with Hollywood Odeon-style curves, the overall effect being one of rather sinister excess and decadence. At the same time, the 'grey furniture' appeared to contend that these 'kitsch' forms were as much a part of the language of contemporary design and culture as the clean-cut, hi-tech forms of more conventional consumer products. Though only ever produced as prototypes, this was furniture with something to say, design that commented on design – 'meta-design' as

The 'Planet as Festival' lithographs of 1972, Sottsass's attempt to visualize buildings 'conserving memories, provoking smiles, boredom eroticism or mysticism etc.'

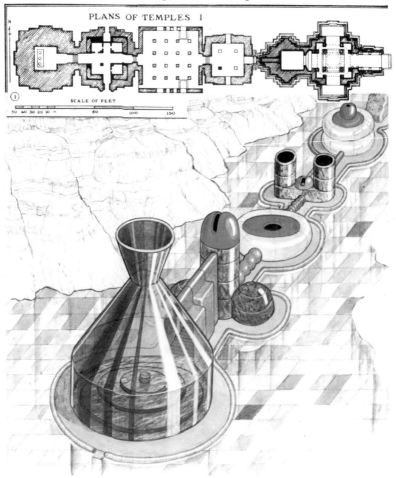

PLANS OF TEMPLES I

SCALE OF FEET

50 40 30 20 10 0   50   100   150

117

Micro-environment designed for the New Domestic Landscape exhibition in New York in 1972. Using technology to gain control over one's own environment was, again, his theme.

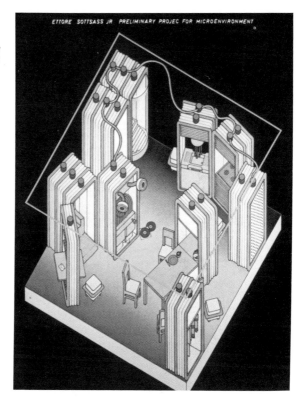

it later came to be called. It undermined the idea of the neutrality of objects, demonstrating instead their emotive and allusive power. Consumption and possession, Sottsass seemed to be saying, were not so simple. Objects did not bring about liberation from history; rather, they bound you to it and reminded you of a continuous cycle of materialist aspirations.

Freedom from the domination of objects was represented by 'The Planet as Festival', Sottsass's 1972 version of the architectural groups' utopian environments. The project consisted of a series of lithographs depicting landscapes inspired by Eastern religious and Western Pop imagery. They are the background to an ideal way of life in which people express their creativity

125

and indulge their imaginative fantasies in an infinitely flexible environment, changing it to suit their moods and activities. The total freedom of this utopia derives from the success of advanced technology which has removed the need to work. This may seem paradoxical in view of Sottsass's mistrust of industrial culture but he emphasizes that he has never been anti-technology.

'I believe very much in technology,' he says, 'but we should not be taken in by its rhetoric. The most important technology is our own lives and it is very important that we should balance it against other needs and problems.' Technology as a means of gaining control over one's own environment was also symbolized in the 'micro-environment' he designed for 'The New Domestic Landscape' exhibition of Italian design at New York's Museum of Modern Art in 1972. This consisted of a series of modules, grey plastic again, each containing different functional elements like a kitchen, WC, sleeping unit etc. In this vision of the future, individuals would arrange their surroundings to suit their way of life, rather than the other way round.

Liberation from the tyranny of objects was also the aim of the designs for Olivetti which Sottsass continued to produce throughout the years of radical design. Technology was again a crucial tool in bringing about greater freedom, this time for workers who spent most of their lives in impersonal and frequently alienating offices. Sottsass saw the design of office equipment as the task of creating an environment dedicated to a particular purpose. The principle was the same, though the purpose was different, as in his 1965 interior design project, 'A Room to Make Love in'; human needs and activities, he thought, should always determine the shape of an environment and objects should be subservient to the requirements of their user.

Although he did design individual pieces of equipment, like a series of typewriters culminating with the Valentine in 1969, his approach is best expressed by the GE 115 computer system of 1966 or the Synthesis office system that he developed between 1968 and 1973. Comprising everything from desks and cabinets to

Sottsass's title of 'A Room to Make Love In' (right) for an exhibition at the Palazzo Strozzi in Florence, in 1965, was censored by the organizers and omitted from the official catalogue. The Olivetti Synthesis office system of 1980-82 (below) offers the possibility of a large variety of layouts for different spaces and environments.

screens and stationery trays, Synthesis provides a neutral, non-oppressive setting that conveys a feeling of calmness and harmony through soft colours and unobtrusive components. Individual pieces like the bright yellow secretary's chair with its Mickey Mouse feet add element of fun and humanistic friendliness . Describing what he was aiming at in this project, Sottsass said, 'We thought we should exercise a sort of "yoga" on design, liberating shape as much as allowed us by our condition in time and space, and stripping from it every attribute, every sex-appeal deception.'

As always, Sottsass was assisted in the fulfillment of

The Olivetti typing chair of 1972, bright yellow with 'Mickey Mouse' feet introduced fun and 'user friendliness' into the office environment.

Carlo Scarpa's Olivetti showroom in the northern portico of St.Mark's Square, Venice, designed in 1958 epitomizes the company's enlightened and intelligent architectural patronage.

his objectives by Adriano Olivetti who was acutely conscious of his company's potential to affect the social and cultural environment. He was particularly aware of their role as 'taste-makers' and it was not simply for prestige but to promote public appreciation of good architecture that he invited people like Carlo Scarpa, Marco Zanuso and Ignazio Gardella to design the firm's international showrooms.

Of course, the enlightened social policy that lay behind the philanthropic architecture of the 'Borgo Olivetti' complex at Ivrea did not preclude a concern with commercial success. The public relations benefits of being patrons of design were not lost on Adriano Olivetti and were proven by the success of the 'Audio-Visual Juke-Box' touring exhibition system that Sottsass designed with Hans von Klier in 1969. Using a designer like Sottsass who was so interested and in touch with popular, especially youth, culture also

129

produced one of the company's greatest consumer successes, the 'Valentine' typewriter, in 1969.

This little bright red plastic portable with its neat, matching slip-case became one of the first 'designer accessories', a compulsory item to be displayed on the shelves of fashionable young apartments. The posters advertising the 'Valentine' are among the most memorable in Olivetti's influential graphic design tradition. Some of them were Sottsass's idea, as was the brilliant notion of selling the new typewriter in clothes boutiques and record shops to reach a bigger, younger market. He declined to create a successor to the 'Valentine', claiming that he saw no point in extending an idea beyond the original inspiration.

Some of the 'radical' designers who produced their alternative environments and counter-design proposals in the late 60s and early 70s retreated to purely theoretical activity in the mid-70s, having argued themselves into a completely anti-production position. For Sottsass, with his lifelong habit of sketching and projecting ideas and realising them in one form or another,

The new Olivetti office building on the outskirts of Ivrea, designed by Bernasconi, Fiocchi and Nizzoli in 1962. The building was conceived in relation to its landscape setting in the Valle d'Aosta.

Sottsass's 'Audiovisual Jukebox' exhibition system was designed, in 1969, for Olivetti business displays. A prefabricated structure made it easily transportable and 40 spectators, equipped with headphones, could gather round to watch short films.

such a withdrawal was never a probability. He had always used design as a means of expressing ideas; as a result of the radical design movement's challenging and questioning the element of communication which had always been present now became a central aspect of his projects.

In the first half of the 70s, Sottsass's creative activities were intimately connected to the course of his private, emotional life. In 1970, he had fallen dramatically in love with a young Spanish artist, Eulalia Grau. She lived in Barcelona and for the next six years he travelled between their two countries, living like a nomad and wandering with his tent throughout the Pyrenees, thinking, drawing, writing and taking photographs. The gypsy-like existence he led in those years represents an attempt to recapture physical and emotional intensity, to go back to a more fundamental, less materialistic way of living.

'I felt a great need to visit deserted places, mountains, to re-establish a physical tie with the cosmos as the only real environment,' he recalls, and he describes his wanderings as 'a journey to the unknown lands of a planet that in books of astronomy is called "the Earth", a journey of exploration of the planet and of ourselves, a journey over lands not to be tainted with signs of death but with scratches of love, with mounds of stones

131

The bas relief for the 'Valentine', 'an object that one takes along with one as one takes one's jacket shoes and hat...'.

or small pieces of mirror, with strips of paper or puddles of water or stakes of some kind.'

Sottsass's initial, overwhelming pleasure in being so close to nature, in 'living on the skin of a celestial fruit' gradually became more refined. Characteristically, he began to see parallels between the relationships of people to landscapes and to design. When the Cooper-Hewitt Museum in New York invited him to take part in its opening exhibition in 1976, he began to plan the photographic record of his journeys into a more unified programme. The completed work comprises three groups of photographs entitled 'Design for the Rights of Man', 'Design for the Destinies of Man' and 'Design for the Necessities of Animals'. They incorporate 'constructions' made out of simple materials that he carried with him or found en route.

The 1976 exhibition marked the completion of this cycle of photographic journeys and coincided with the ending of his relationships with both Eualaia Grau and Nanda, his wife. But Sottsass continued to travel and with his new lover, Barbara Radice, he made journeys all over the world between 1976 and 1979. These are commemorated in the 'My Fiancee' and 'Decorations' series of photographs, comments on design, existence, cultural aggression and the language of decoration.

This long period of reflection had profound implications for the way in which Sottsass was to approach

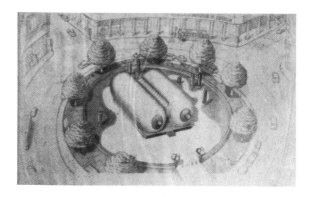

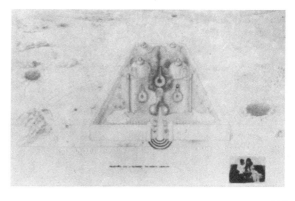

The 'architectural pornography' drawings of 1973 use extreme, and explicit, symbolism to suggest a more communicative architecture. A nursery, for example is placed within two huge 'breasts' (above), while the 'brothel for liberated exercises' is sited amidst structural analogies of various female organs (below).

the design of objects. It encouraged him to think more deeply about the relationship between things and the people using them. 'Today we are far more sober and even suspicious and confrontations occur far more frequently,' he said in 1978. 'The drawings of "architectural pornography" (a 1973 series in which he had sited a nursery school, for example, within two huge breasts and a "brothel for liberated exercises" amidst various female organs), the Planet as Festival, are utopias in which the message is not in the quantity of objects or in their design but in communication. Where does one go? what does one do? what meaning do linguistic symbols have? and so on.' For him, this did not involve giving up design but it encouraged a more wary approach to the process.

De Pas , D'Urbino and Lomazzi's 'Blow' sofa for Zanotta, 1967. This transparent Pvc seating was an experimental idea that was enthusiastically taken up by consumers bored with 'good taste'.

'There is definitely more cautiousness, circumspection, care and attention. Today I create much less than I did in the past, and not only because I have grown older. If today somebody comes to me for a new lighting fixture, we will work on it for at least two to three months. There was a time when I would have known at once what this fixture should look like. It was enough to know what the product was supposed to do and what were the production facilities and – avanti. Today I am not sure I know what to do and in which style to work. The relationship with the public which is going to use the product has grown

Aldo Branzi's Muzio sidetable for Studio Alchymia, 1979.

so complex (or maybe I have become more aware of its innate complexity) that I simply don't know how to touch people I am not familiar with.'

Apart from his work for Olivetti, Sottsass designed few objects for industrial production in the 1970s. He wanted to communicate the idea that design could act as comment and criticism; it need not denote slavish acceptance of the capitalist system of production, selling and consumption in which objects were simply the means of sustaining demand and ensuring profits. Often, this meant designing objects that would never be manufactured, at least within an industrial context , but Sottsass believes that design can be highly influential and significant without going into production. He refers to Aldo Rossi, an architect whom he greatly admires, as someone who had a powerful effect through his drawings and projects before any of his designs were actually built; conversely, the Bauhaus had a good influence on designers' thinking but there are, as he points out, some terrible results, particularly in the area of public housing, of uncomprehending attempts to translate Bauhaus theories into buildings.

Although manufacturers like Zanotta and even Cassina had produced some pieces of radical furniture design such as Lomazzi, D'Urbino and De Pas's 'Blow' sofa and Paolo Deganello's 'Aeo' chair, most experimental work remained in two dimensions with the occasional prototype being made up by individual craftsmen. Studio Alchymia was different – a 'workshop' that produced radical design intended for production. It had been set up as a 'radical' graphic design studio by Alessandro Guerriero in 1976 but two years later he helped to make an exhibition of furniture by Alessandro Mendini, the editor of *Casabella* in its radical early 70s mode and then editor of both *Domus* and *Modo*. Through Mendini, Guerriero met Sottsass and the ex-Superstudio architect, Andrea Branzi; he invited them to join Studio Alchymia and form a group dedicated to research and innovative environmental design. The younger architects, Michele De Lucchi and Paola Navone were also members of the group.

Sottsass had already formed his own studio but he

welcomed the opportunity to participate in this forum for discussion and design. He had worked with Branzi on a series of furniture and lamps for the retail chain Croff Casa, the Italian Habitat, in 1977-78. These colourful but quite subdued and simple pieces were an attempt to introduce 'communicative' furniture into the general domestic environment but dismal sales figures indicated that the average consumer was not sufficiently responsive to the designers' message to ponder it in their living room. According to Barbara Radice, 'salesmen actually discouraged clients from

'The Structures Tremble', 1979. Part of Sottsass's Studio Alchymia collection that projected a new approach to 'conceptual furniture'.

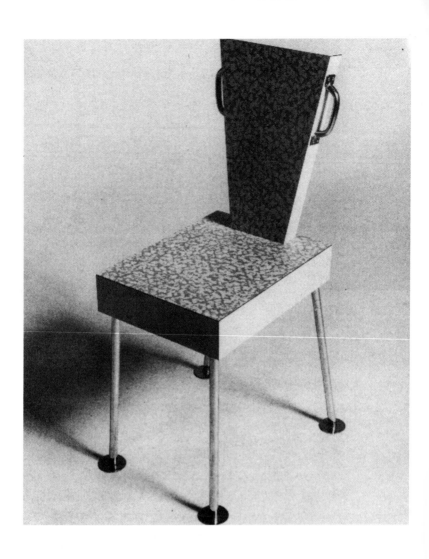

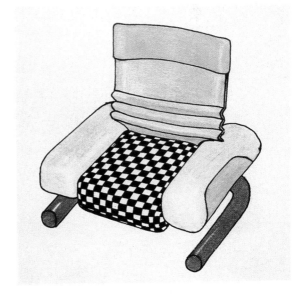

Sottsass's dining chair for Studio Alchymia (left) introduced print plastic laminate as a furnishing material. Alessandro Mendini's 'Kandissy' sofa (above) reinterpreted a traditional form with references to modern art, while Michelle De Lucchi's 'Peter Pan' 'dressing up' chair (right) added fun to modernist styling.

buying the pieces'; whether this was for reasons of personal taste or doubt about the furniture's durability is not specified.

The Studio Alchymia exhibitions of 1979 and 1980 did not elicit much more enthusiasm from the design fraternity though they did attract a lot of attention from a rather sceptical media and socialites anxious to be au fait with the avant garde. The different positions of the three principal designers emerged clearly at these shows: with his series of 'redesigns', Mendini, the creator of the 'Kandissi' (Kandinsky) sofa and 'Proust' armchair, expressed doubt that design was capable of doing anything new or effecting any change in attitudes; Branzi's reinterpretations of Modern Movement forms indicated a less pessimistic outlook while Sottsass and De Lucchi introduced a completely new conceptual and aesthetic approach.

The inspiration and imagery of their Alchymia furniture and objects combined characteristics of the urban public environment and the suburban domestic landscape. Some of the forms recalled the 1950s when

Andrea Branzi, Sottsass's collaborator in Studio Alchymia, explored the use of materials like bamboo and wood in experimental collections like 'Domestic Animals', 1985.

140

Italian design was still dedicated to the creation of a new visual personality for a new society but the references were too wide-ranging for the collections to be labelled nostalgia. The materials were deliberately selected from the zone of 'non-culture'; they included 'the grit and mosaics of public conveniences in the underground stations of big cities, the tight wire netting of suburban fences, the spongy paper of government account books' – and plastic laminate, 'a material with no uncertainties'.

For Sottsass, the Alchymia designs were a more dramatic attempt than his Croff Casa range to present a collection of popular furniture; but to justify that definition they had to be capable of being manufactured and made available to consumers, not just of brief exposure to a knowing elite. Guerriero and Branzi were almost entirely preoccupied with experimental exhibitions and cultural polemics and it became clear that Studio Alchymia would not be the nest from which a new species, capable of flight into the world beyond, would emerge. Sottsass would have to look for a launching pad elsewhere.

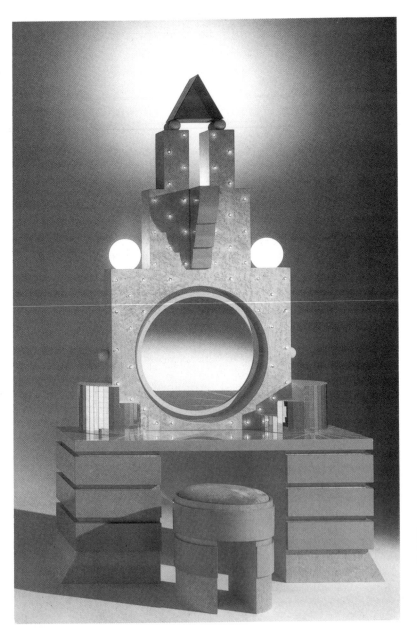

from memphis to malibu

The Via Borgonuovo in Milan is a quiet, shady street between the fashionable shopping area of Via Montenapoleone and the tranquil Brera district that surrounds the picture gallery and fine art academy. Behind the heavy 19th century facade of number nine is a typical Milanese courtyard overlooked by the offices and studios of Sottsass Associates. There is little to distinguish these airy white interiors from the city's scores of other architectural practices until one looks at the drawing boards and the few visuals pinned on the studio walls. Here are the drawings of all kinds that, according to Sottsass, 'somehow represent that great number of anxious hours spent together every day trying to understand where we were going and where we would end up, and to represent the innumerable thoughts usually hidden or forgotten which instead serve as an intellectual binder between one decision and another; as a binder for the entire period of time.'

Sottsass Associati was founded in May 1980 by Sottsass and three much younger, newly-qualified architects . To the many sceptics who expressed doubts about his partners' experience, he responded, 'I have always worked with very young people. When I was young nobody gave me any work or opportunities. I knew I could have done outstanding things and I have always remembered that. I also know that people in certain conditions (the question is to understand the conditions) can do things that nobody would ever have suspected. I believe the young are more honest and sensitive, more doubtful and less conceited than the old.

The 'Plaza' dressing table by American architect Michael Graves for the 1981 Memphis collection, uses maple root, lacquered wood, mirror , glass and brass to construct a lavish, near-parody of the Memphis idea.

143

They're not all like that, but... these boys looked honest and keen.'

The first of his three partners was Marco Zanini who, like himself, came from the Dolomites. Zanini had been a friend since meeting Sottsass at a Global Tools workshop in 1975, when he was a second year student at the School of Architecture in Florence. In spite of an age difference of well over 30 years, the two men were strongly in sympathy with each others' ideas and they continue to work together closely on a wide range of projects.

Of the other two partners, Matteo Thun, an aristocratic Tyrolean, had been a fellow student of Zanini's while Aldo Cibic, a large, sociable Venetian studied design in Vicenza. Thun and Cibic have both now left to set up their own studios and Thun is already extremely successful. Many other young designers from all over the world have come to the Via Borgonuovo, some have stayed, and the office now numbers about 25, with a separate graphics group run by Christoph Radl. The group functions in a non-hierarchical and flexible manner; many members work on a freelance

Ettore Sottsass at his office in the Via Borgonuovo, Milan in November 1990.

Via Borgonuovo 9

basis but everyone has the opportunity to contribute to office policy. There is a high level of communication between teams of designers and other collaborators; as Sottsass says, 'We don't see this goal of raising the quality of life as a solitary, personal act. We think the possibility of existing with others is part of the quality of contemporary life.'

1980 was a significant year. Sottsass Associates had been formed in May and, as the world now knows, Memphis was born some months later. That autumn, the carpenter Renzo Brugola, an old friend and collaborator who had worked with Sottsass on his furniture for Poltronova in the 60s, suggested that they should get together for a new joint venture. And Mario and Brunella Godani, who owned a smart store in the centre of Milan, asked him if they could sell some of his new furniture in their shop. A year later, Sottsass asked these acquaintances if they would produce and exhibit, respectively, a show of 'very up-to-date' furniture designed by himself and some 'very clever friends'. Both agreed readily but it was not until mid-December that the 'Memphis' label emerged as a title for the collection.

There were absolutely no formal or stylistic guidelines for this new furniture. The December '80 discussions in Sottsass's flat or at a nearby pizzeria, attended by Michelle De Lucchi, Marco Zanini, Matteo Thun, Aldo Cibic, Martine Bedin, George Sowden, Natalie du Pasquier, Barbara Radice and Sottsass himself centred round ideas, intentions and iconography rather than forms and materials. Thus the name Memphis was seized upon, as Bob Dylan's *Memphis Blues* played on Sottsass's record player, since it seemed to symbolize an eclectic, clashing, emotive combination of ancient Egypt with American suburbs and rock'n'roll.

The ambiguity of the Memphis label was appropriate, if fortuitous. It precisely conveyed the group's simultaneous celebration of high and low culture and the unlimited nature of the sources from which they took their inspiration. The first drawings of 'New Design' furniture were produced in February 1981 and somehow, over the course of the next seven, frantic,

(Overleaf) Project drawings produced at Sottsass Associates

145

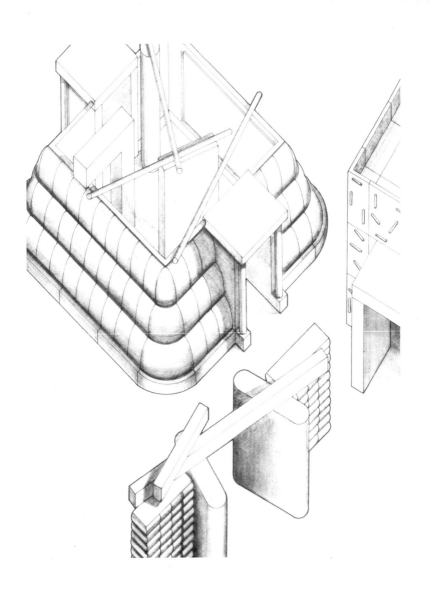

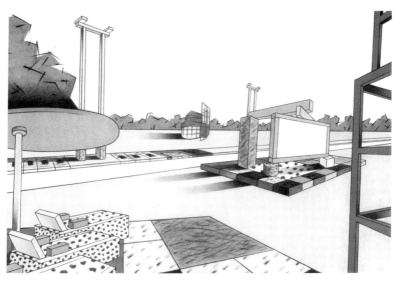

months the furniture, lamps, ceramics, fabrics and clocks that comprised the first Memphis collection were designed and produced in time for a mid-September opening attended by two and a half thousand people.

The curious crowds who flocked to that first exhibition included design journalists from all over the world and they naturally tried to come up with a definition that would convey what Memphis was all about. Inevitably, they described it as a 50's revival, a 30's revival, a homage to kitsch, a form of neo-classicism. None of these definitions came close to explaining what Memphis was really about, though each contained an element of truth. In spite of the very open nature of the Memphis design 'programme', there was a coherent message expressed by all the works in the exhibition, though not one that could be described in terms of a style label.

The problems and objectives tackled by the Memphis designers were those that Sottsass had been considering for years. They were linguistic, as much as aesthetic, challenges in that the objects attempted to reverse the scale of values attached to certain words, particularly

The original partners of Sottsass Associates, founded in May 1980. Front row, left to right: Matteo Thun, Marco Zanini, Ettore Sottsass, Aldo Cibic.

those describing materials. In producing luxury living room furniture finished in the plastic laminates associated with kitchens and bathrooms, they were indirectly drawing the attention of the public to a hierarchy of materials. This was, says Sottsass, a 'political action', in that they were inviting people to consider how status was endowed by words like gold or marble. 'I wanted to take away the defence given by the conventional scale of values to a certain political group. A rich woman covered in gold, for example, can say that she has the best, because gold is the best. Instead, Memphis was saying that you are the best if you have plastic laminate.'

As this indicates, Sottsass saw Memphis less as a group of products than as a collection of 'philosophical notes and statements'. For him, it represented research, which people could be affected by without having to possess the objects. This was his response to those who said that, because of the high cost of the items, Memphis was only available to the rich. As ever, for Sottsass, the

The staff of the Sottsass Associates studio in 1988.

149

Designers of the Memphis group in Masanori Umeda's 'Tawaraya' ring, 1981.

communication of ideas to a wider environment was more important than the mass production of objects. 'A good design is like the possibility of going to the moon,' he explains. 'Few people will have the opportunity to experience it directly but its existence will change the lives of millions.'

Memphis's lavish, unexpected and rather shocking use of plastic laminates was the most significant expressive element within the communications system that their designs represented. Not only did it suggest a new hierarchy of materials but it indicated the possibility of a new approach to culture which encouraged a wider awareness and a broadening of ideas about creative expression. The vibrant, jazzy laminates that had previously been confined to coffee bars, fast-food restaurants and working-class homes in first, second and third-world suburbia were now applied to large, elegant and expensive pieces of furniture that were only suitable for large, elegant rooms in affluent interiors. They were thus transplanted from a realm of vulgarity and 'bad taste' to a world of refinement and 'good taste', upsetting a number of orthodoxies and preconceptions in the process.

150

Designers, and consumers, said Memphis with its plastic laminates, must look beyond the glossy magazines and city centre showrooms in their pursuit of a new visual language. The exuberant patterns, lurid colours and fake textures of tower block kitchens were as valid an expression of contemporary culture as the minimalist forms and subdued surfaces of 'classic', modern functionalist design. It was not substituting a new style; rather it was revealing new possibilities and new alliances between design and culture. As Michelle De Lucchi has said, 'We are trying to connect design and industry to the broader culture within which we move.'

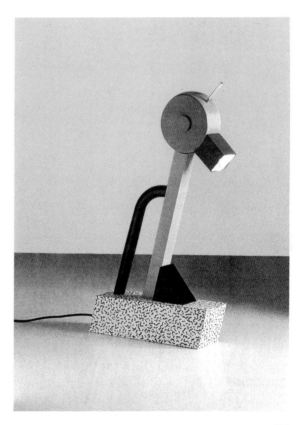

Sottsass's 'Tahiti' lamp for Memphis, 1981. The combination of print laminate and metal represented an early example of uniting 'high' and 'low' materials, decoration and function.

Memphis plastic laminates made an original statement in characteristically original language. The patterns and textures the designers invented were inspired by a mixture of popular decorative graphics, fine art stereotypes and organic forms. The impact of this new language of surface ornament was so great that many of the designs were soon transferred to other materials and began to appear on sweatshirts, shoes and wrapping paper as well as bookcases, beds and wardrobes.

Other materials were also subjected to the Memphis shaking-up of dormant sensibilities. Static, predictable applications and juxtapositions of precious, synthetic and industrial materials were rejected and reassembled,

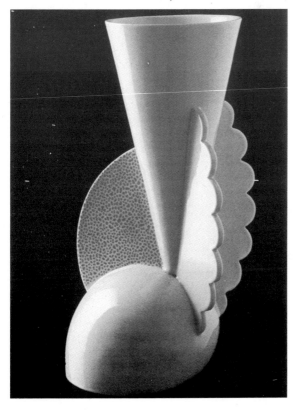

Matteo Thun's 'Onega' cup for the 1982 Memphis collection dares to decorate virginal white porcelain.

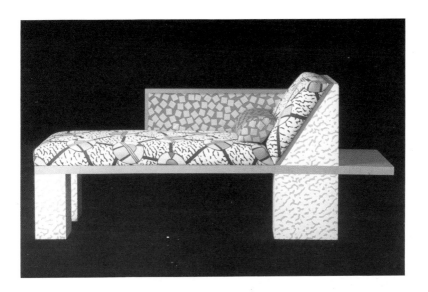

Nathalie du Pasquier's 'Royal' Memphis sofa, 1983, covered in print laminate and printed cotton. Du Pasquier was the prolific designer of an endless variety of prints for fabrics and laminates.

so that cheap coloured light bulbs were attached to marble dresser tops and aluminium was inlaid with mother-of-pearl. It was another means of suggesting greater potential, similar, said Sottsass, to the invasion of civilized societies by barbarians with their 'nonculture'. Also, people's direct sensual responses to familiar materials were revitalized when they encountered them taken out of predictable contexts and relationships. Uninhibited and anarchic combinations of cheap and expensive, coarse and sophisticated materials made each piece of Memphis furniture a rich, sometimes confusing rearrangement of conventional material vocabulary.

The Memphis attitude to decoration and colour was equally questioning and irreverent. Instead of seeing decoration as something separate from and imposed upon a structure, Sottsass claimed that 'A Memphis table *is* decoration. Structure and decoration are one thing.' Rather than being considered as an isolated element, decoration was a fundamental part of the design process that produced Memphis objects. The random, autonomous shapes and patterns were generated in the same way as ideas and forms for individual

'Gabon', from Nathalie du Pasquier's 1982 range of fabrics, inspired by African textile art.

products. Colour, similarly, was treated as an integral part of a design and was an active ingredient of the final mix.

There is no particular Memphis palette; different designers tended to use different ranges of colour, but they shared Sottsass's desire to jettison conventional applications and discover a new, unfettered response. As he explains it, 'I've always looked for nonculturised colour in the colours of children, and I've always drawn a blank because nobody understands this way of treating colour...Now that we have been through that experience and got rid of our inhibitions, so to speak, we can do almost anything we want. We can even allow ourselves a more cultivated, more sophisticated colour, because we know how to use it in a loose, detached way as though it had no links with any culture.'

In spite of its explosive impact and universal imitations, Memphis was never intended or presented as a new style of design. It actually opposed the notion of style, as in 'the International Style', as an artificial and inhibiting orthodoxy. Instead, it proposed a more open and flexible design culture, one that Andrea Branzi described as 'actively engaged in the reconstruction of a system of expressive and emotional relations between man and the objects of his domestic habitat, reaching out from design to architecture and the city.'

The fundamental idea, of design as communication, and the objective of arriving at a closer correspondence between design and culture, clearly stemmed from Sottsass's continuing commitment to design as a liberating means of expression. Sensual liberation, rather than intellectual or ideological satisfaction, is what he was always aiming to provide. 'I am an idiot,' he has said, ' and I've always said the problem is to eat, drink, sex, sleep and stay down low, low, low. The world is an area of sensory recovery...World culture today is concerned with the American vision of comfort. ..To have money means to possess sensory possibilities, not power. Sensoriality destroys ideology, it is anarchical, private; it takes account of consumerism and consumption, it is not moralistic, it opens up new avenues.'

Memphis echoed a scepticism about functionalism, so-called, that Sottsass had indicated in 1954. 'When Charles Eames designs his chair, he does not design just a chair,' he said. 'He designs a way of sitting down. In other words, he designs a function, not for a function.' With the younger Memphis designers he inspired, Sottsass too was designing a function for objects. Beyond a few basic provisions, their furniture was fulfilling a new function, that of the expression and communication of cultural states and values.

The overthrow of rigid definitions of good taste and acceptable visual references was welcomed and embraced beyond all expectations. Inevitably, most of the imitations that appeared immediately and every-

The coveted invitation to the Memphis exhibition in September
1981 (top). Lack of it did not deter the crowd of two and a half
thousand who turned up to see what it was all about (above). The book
of the movement (right) followed in 1983.

MEMPHIS

The New International Style

MARTINE BEDIN   ANDREA BRANZI   ALDO CIBIC   MICHELE DE LUCCHI
NATHALIE DU PASQUIER MICHAEL GRAVES HANS HOLLEIN ARATA ISOZAKI
TERRY JONES SHIRO KURAMATA JAVIER MARISCAL ALESSANDRO MENDINI
PAOLA NAVONE PETER SHIRE ETTORE SOTTSASS GEORGE JAMES SOWDEN
STUDIO ALCHYMIA MATTEO THUN MASANORI UMEDA MARCO ZANINI

where, lacked the substance and devalued the significance of the original. In that way, it recalled the cycle of fashion design and began to be identified as a fashion. The designers were less upset by this than might have been imagined. Indeed, in her introduction to the first Memphis catalogue in 1981, Barbara Radice had written, 'We are all sure that Memphis furniture will soon go out of style.' And Sottsass had stated, 'Today everything one does is consumed. It is dedicated to life, not to eternity.'

Though it generated its collectors, Memphis furniture was never intended to be a series of one-off pieces, far less a collection of art objects. It was conceived from the outset in terms of industrial production, seen as a means of exploiting industry's most up-to-date methods of distribution, sales and flexible production systems. In spite of Sottsass's insistence that mass production is not necessary for the effective dissemination of ideas, the group were not interested in rejecting industrial production in order to return to some nostalgic and marginal form of craft production. In the event, industry, and possibly the designers themselves, were not quite flexible enough to produce the diversity and originality they required. Memphis furniture, as such, was never produced cheaply enough to be affordable for a mass audience but furniture shops and living rooms throughout the western world were nevertheless affected, via cheaper imitations, by its liberating vocabulary of colour and materials. If nothing else, it made furniture shopping fun, thus fulfilling Sottsass's aim of introducing a dimension of sensory pleasure to a necessary ritual of contemporary life, consumerism.

The 'long period of conceptual preparation' that culminated in the creation of objects for Alchymia and Memphis, was also a time of thinking and discussion about how to do architecture.

The graphics division of Sottsass Associates is now run by Christoph Radl who designed these logos in 1982 and 1983. The second from the top is by Valentina Grego, 1983.

Sottsass Associates, says its founder, 'enlarged' the work of Memphis into interiors and buildings, as well as industrial products and mass produced domestic objects that grew out of the simultaneous development of ideas and research. The last 'official' Memphis show was in

1987. 'The Memphis iconography has been vigorously tested, worked, manipulated, multiplied, perhaps even consumed and exhausted,' says Sottsass. 'But it is certain that the Memphis intellectual premises have also been re-tested, recorded, reinvented and reused in large scale operations, not in ordinary objects or furniture any more but in complicated and vast architectural settings, in elaborate and intense design situations.'

The industrial design output of Sottsass Associates is unexpectedly large and formidably specialized. As well as the more predictable telephones (for Enorme) and hairdryers (for Welonda), there have been modular control systems for machine tools, robots, and a 'non-stop working centre' for mechanical and electronic parts. The design of these high technology products for factory automation exploits new technologies to develop expressive, user-friendly forms. In that sense, their function, to relate to consumers, is identical to that of interiors and furniture

Ironically, in view of Sottsass's identification of design with politics, one of the first urban and architectural commissions awarded to Sottsass Associates, street

Printed plastic laminates 'Rete' and 'Spugnato' designed by Ettore Sottsass (above left), 'Fantastic' and 'Micidial' by Michelle De Lucchi (above right). De Lucchi's 'Pacific' wardrobe, 1981, (facing) combines jazzy printed laminate with cool metal and glass.

furniture for the City of Turin, was swept away with the Socialist Vice-Mayor who had initiated the project. Elements of the design system were retained and some, like parts of the kiosks, have been installed. But commissions carried out for, and with, private clients have been more successful.

The group's attitude to and relationship with clients is probably unique. It is certainly not, as Sottsass says,

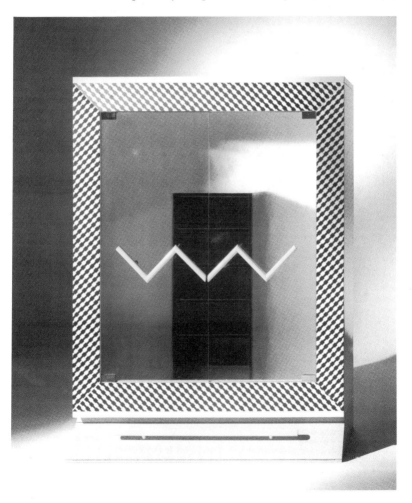

'The attitude of two sides of the table.' He describes the evolution of a project thus: 'First we get to know the people who approach us to do a project very well. We discuss not only work, but also life, politics, lovers, families, food, clothes. We have terrible fights and sometimes we go with them on trips to Polynesia or the Colorado mountains. Together with them, we circulate the water of culture.' It is a very different approach from most of today's international architects. 'I am not Norman Foster - I don't have a helicopter,' says Sottsass, but he thinks that different schools of architecture will co-exist in the modern world. There will be the well-organized architectural businesses and other people like himself and his partners, producing architecture of 'another density' and a smaller scale.

The Sottsass Associates collaboration with Doug Tompkins, founder of the Esprit chain of clothes shops, is the best and most prolonged example of how they operate with and for clients. Tompkins first met Sottsass socially, at the urging of a mutual friend, and they spent a pleasant day discussing anything but business. A year later, when he was looking for someone to carry out a series of interiors projects, he called on Sottsass in Milan to see if he could recommend some designers. After a long meeting, he unreservedly appointed Sottsass Associates and, 'It was then that an extensive and intensive relationship began.'

After two years of frequent, often lengthy visits to Milan, staying at Aldo Cibic's flat and occupying a

place in the office, Tompkins became 'just another body around the studio':'Slowly over time, my presence was less and less considered that of the client. As in most professional environments, work and personal life merge into one. Within the studio, days were full of constant design discussion over lunch, dinner, or often late into the night. More and more of a personal philosophy of social living began to be formulated about the work and our own points of view. Slowly a new quality seemed to emerge from the work. The

Peter Shire's 'Bel Air' armchair for the Memphis 1982 collection. Most of the pieces were named after places considered exotic for one reason or another.

distance that often exists between client and architect, student and teacher, buyer and seller, fell away and an entirely different relationship appeared...what I have found is that in the realm of custom design, this constant communication, give and take, interplay of ideas, needs, taste and requirements leads to a much higher degree of quality in the final product.' (quoted in *Sottsass Associates*, Rizzoli 1988)

Tompkins does acknowledge the disadvantages of increased costs and time delays, the clashes of taste and opinion, that accompany such intense collaboration. 'The iconography and signature of the Sottsass studio... is extremely strong, directional and particular,' he

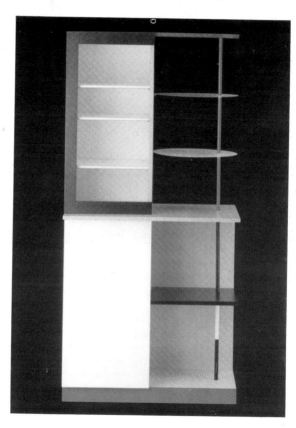

Gerard Taylor's 'Airport' cabinet, 1982, in print laminate and metal. Taylor, a Scottish designer, was one of Sottsass's many young international associates.

Sottsass's Memphis glass objects have become some of the most collectible and coveted items of the group's collections. The 'Alioth' and 'Alcor' blown glass vases (above left and right) and 'Sirio' (facing) were produced by the craftsmen of Toso Vetri d'Arte, Murano in 1982.

concedes. 'It is important that this sensibility be left to its own visual expression.' But he prefers to emphasize the high level of satisfaction they all shared with the fifteen projects completed by Sottsass Associates for Esprit and he describes the association as 'an incredible learning process'.

'For me, it has been somewhat akin to graduate school,' he explains. 'Working with a great master, learning about open- ended thinking (which is the only way I know to describe Ettore's reasoning process) has been sensational. Learning, as we all have, about integrating social, political, sexual, natural, and mystical elements into solutions to design problems has given me the greatest satisfaction with my client/architect

Sottsass Associates developed this multi-coloured telephone for Enorme Corporation, a small company specialising in futuristic versions of household and office utensils.

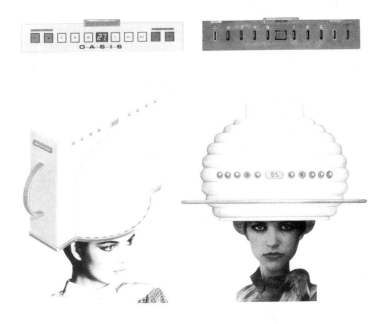

relationship. I think I can also speak for Marco and Aldo, Ettore's partners, as well as for anyone working closely within the studio, that we've all benefited by this master/apprentice relationship. It is the reason for many that they are there at all. Along with that comes an internationalism that is certainly enriched by the mix of different nationalities within the studio - designers from America, England, Japan, France, Austria, and elsewhere all come together to search for the same thing - a slice of the wisdom of the maestro.' (ibid.)

The showrooms and shops for Esprit in Dusseldorf, Zurich, Hamburg, Berlin, Vienna and other cities are all strikingly theatrical, though highly functional, spaces. They provide optimum facilities for displaying and storing the clothes as well as for the incorporation of sophisticated point-of-sale and computer ordering technology. Entrances and staircases act as preludes

The Welonda hairdryer prototypes of 1981 typify the Sottsass Associates approach of devising new, expressive forms for familiar objects.

to the drama of the shopping spaces and specially designed architectural elements create atmospheric interiors, sometimes suggestive of the past, sometimes of the future.

For a site next to the store in San Francisco, Esprit's headquarters, Sottsass Associates designed *Snaporazz*, a restaurant named after the Marcello Mastroianni character in Fellini's *City of Women*. The project architects, Sottsass and Marco Zanini, created an interior which emphasized the sensual experience of eating simple Italian and Californian-American food. An integrated sushi bar was designed by Sottsass's friend, the Japanese architect Shiro Kuramata but the project was eventually abandoned in favour of a more basic cafe concept.

The restaurant was broken up into several sections, large, small, high and low, and each overlooks a theme garden - the tropical garden, Zen garden, marble garden and a hothouse cactus garden. This one project, comprised a series of fragmentary experiences represented by, for instance, a miniature cypress wood, a Mediterranean pergola and a scaled-down hi-tech tower. Such fragmentation is typical of Sottsass's attitude to history, 'whatever it may be'. 'All things considered,' he says, 'we don't really know what history is... I believe there is an idea of history as it was before the Greeks or as it was at the time of ancient India or maybe as it now is on the island of Malekula...people were not living, are not living to enter the gate of history; they seem to have wanted, if anything to enter the gate of memory... there were and are memories to keep life company; memories to be archived more as long songs, or as long stories to tell, or as gossip, or as examples to amaze people with...' Or, perhaps, as architecture which prefers to evoke memories than build monuments.

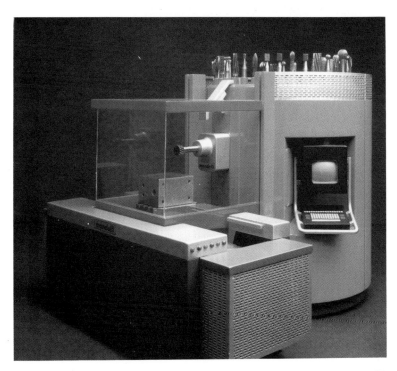

The Esprit projects successfully vindicate Sottsass's insistence that Sottsass Associates can only design for clients who are friends. Because of their friendship with Tompkins, the designers were aware of the type of market, environment and merchandise that appealed to Esprit customers. They were thus able, as Sottsass describes it, 'to create designs for a specific ritual - places for happy, modern serene people with a certain idea about morality, life and sport. Knowing the kind of people, we were able to produce a shell for the event and fit it with furnishings that developed the Memphis idea.'

The other criterion for accepting a commission is that they will be allowed to work in total freedom. In the case of the Wolf House in Colorado, the brief was 'so free it was almost negative.' The client, a friend of Sottsass's curator friend at the Metropolitan Museum in New York, had seen his work there and liked it so much that he asked Sottsass to build him 'a most beautiful house'. 'It can be whatever you want,' he added, 'but it must be a work of architecture.'

The house, with its flowing spaces, variety of forms and close relationship between the building and its natural surroundings is certainly that. It is also a colourful, functional, stimulating environment, specifically designed for a particular individual but expressing both European and American culture. The furniture has

These 1981 kiosks (below and facing), were designed by Sottsass Associates as one element in a co-ordinated urban furniture system for the City of Turin. The low-cost, modular system, based on extensive research gave a definite architectural identity to newspaper kiosks and souvenir stands, bus shelters and public conveniences.

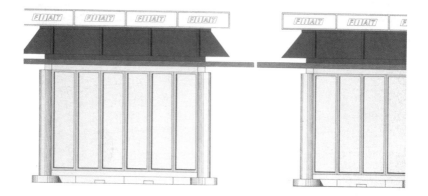

Newsstand Type Kiosk

26

173

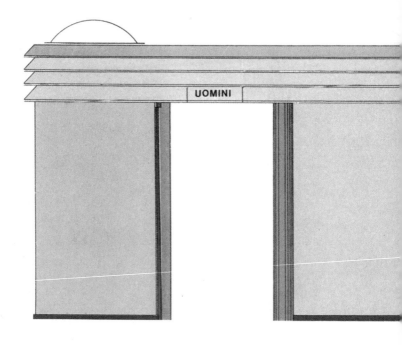

UOMINI

been made by Sottsass's old friend and associate, the carpenter Renzo Brugola. It brings to the house a sense of quality which is quintessentially Italian while the simple materials and ranch-style structure try to 'recuperate American memories'. The house itself, in fact, 'is a very small part of the project'. 'All the rest is its surroundings', says Sottsass. 'There are many different places to hide, stay, look. It represents an approach to solving problems one after the other, not in a once and for all way.'

Another house, the Palevsky home in Malibu, incorporates the atmosphere of both ancient seaside villas

One of the kiosks that have been installed in Turin is seen above. The vicissitudes of local politics meant that the system was never carried out in its entirety.

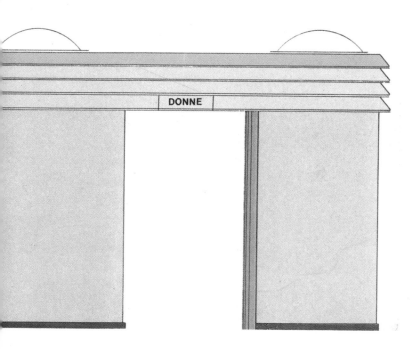

and contemporary pop culture, while a small apartment building in Massa in central Italy, 'tells stories of Ligurian and perhaps Tuscan memories'. Of simple and traditional construction, it makes exquisite use of materials such as local marble, sandstone and copper. Nestling within coastal forest, the house is pinky-white and pale blue and, say the designers, 'When, after a while, the wind and sun have faded and sprinkled it with pine-needles, it will look as if it had always been there as, we hope, a happy part of the landscape.'

These houses, with their accretionary approach to design, seem to symbolize a reconciling of Sottsass's

The Esprit shop in Cologne (left) incorporates flights of pink marble staircase, 'conceived as a closed tunnel leading to the different acts and scenes that will unfold before visitors' eyes'. The Zurich showroom (right) reproduces the concept of an Italian small town whose focal point is the piazza.

The Zurich showroom (left) divides spaces by architectural elements like the huge window between cafeteria and entrance hall. The Dusseldorf showroom (right) is an open plan space with specially designed architectural elements like lacquered iron 'pergola' structures.

training as an architect with his experiments as a designer. Apart from being too poor, before, to open an architectural studio, the cultural and psychological conditions did not seem appropriate for doing bigger things, like buildings. Now he is ready to try, but *his* skyscraper, for example, will not be a huge monolithic unit: 'It will be like a piece of furniture, broken into many small spaces, maybe not even finished.' The monolithic ideological approach cannot work, he believes, because the world contains too many 'suppositions'. 'It is like a big desert with high dunes and you see quite different landscapes depending on whether you are on top of or below the dunes.'

The rich mingling of temporal and geographical memories that occurs in his architecture recalls his own long voyages to the East and West. His journeys to India, America, Polynesia have convinced him of the need to create a 'planetarian' culture rather than prolonging nationalistic attitudes: 'Today we have to work together to develop an attitude that permits different tribes to live together under the general umbrella of the planet. Instead of comparing ourselves to others or trying to be missionaries, we should be opening communications with others.'

Everything, thinks Sottsass, can be discussed, made

The Snaporazz restaurant project for the Esprit headquarters, in 1984-85, in San Francisco was an environment designed as a series of buildings relating to the gardens. Each part of the restaurant looked out onto a different themed garden.

The Snaporazz dining areas represented numerous different situations, large, small, open or closed with high or low ceilings.

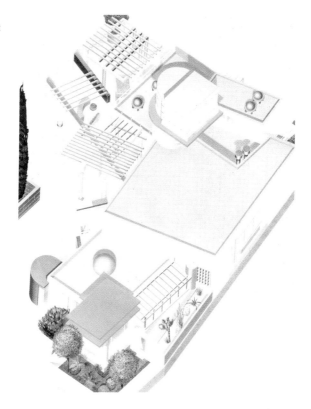

compatible and put in a relationship with other things. Technology is an important example, something which must be accepted, even welcomed, but controlled and put in balance so that it enriches, rather than destroys, life. The time for aggressive words is past, he believes. Now he feels that it is enough just to do little things , whereas in the 60s, designers like himself were almost in a state of ideological war. Not that he has ever felt really aggressive; 'I was like a child, just, always trying to reach the limits of where I could go.' Now this apparent aggression is no longer necessary; through Memphis, a point was made and a change in ideas about design was brought about.

Ettore Sottsass and Marco Zanini, the designers, pictured Snaporazz as 'a sum of fragmentary and diversified experiences'. They included a cypress wood, a Mediterranean pergola and a slightly hi-tech tower (facing above and below). The Fiorucci shop interior in Amsterdam, 1980-83, (right, above and below) ironically combines prehistoric animal frescoes with contemporary human fashion.

Rather than seeing the world, and his work, in terms of points to aim for and reach, Sottsass now sees society as a collection of metaphors. 'We are all conditioned by metaphors so strong that we don't see them as that any more; we live from metaphors every day, seeing paintings in the form of reproductions, architecture in the form of book illustrations. Photographs are metaphors because only the photographer has a true idea of what he is photographing. We relate it to what we know, we see what we know, not necessarily what is there. Even we ourselves are the result of cultural conditions, we are not free but conditioned by stories, memories and metaphors.'

This apartment for Bruno Munari in Venice, 1983, was designed within a traditional Venetian interior with painted ceilings and terrazzo floors. The dining room creates an image of contemporary classicism.

The Munari drawing room
incorporates contemporary
furnishing in a historic setting.

The Munari drawing room incorporates contemporary furnishing in a historic setting.

What this indicates, says Sottsass, is that nobody actually possesses anything very much, in terms of reality. Banks, museums, economic and political powers, build up metaphors about nationalism and tradition that lead to wars; if we reject these, we will become more free, have more respect for others and realize we all need to help, rather than control, each other.

Clearly, this way of thinking originates from Sottsass's experience as a young architect trying to begin his career under Fascism. His questioning of authorities and dogmas of all kinds has persisted since then and continues now. It has inspired remarkably eloquent and expressive design of all kinds and his latest work is making a significant contribution to the popular environment, worldwide. He also, is achieving the recognition and acclaim that his work, comment and

In 1980, Sottsass and Zanini designed a discotheque in a suburb north of Beirut. An upper gallery has a view over the dance floor and a curtain wall facing the sea (above). Sottsass Associates' Office of the Future exhibit for Olivetti, 1983-84, (below) is humanistic hi-tech.

Sottsass designed this house in Colorado for the art dealer and collector, Daniel Wolf, 1986-88. Two main elements are connected by a large atrium room open to the sky. Early sketches (below) show the development of a strong original idea, inspired by a Pompeian fresco.

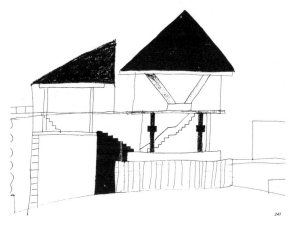

241

influence have long entitled him to, though he remains unaffected by such attention. As he said 20 years ago, all he wants is for everyone to be given the same opportunities for creative self-expression, the same chances to be free to find themselves and their own place in the world:

'There they sit on small or large thrones that they have conquered, or even on kitchen chairs, because they have been told that they are not artists, that they cannot allow themselves to grow their hair, nor to design their own clothes, nor to build their own furniture, nor to make up their own songs, nor to write their own

187

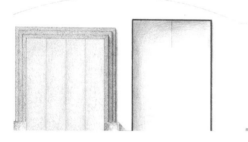

poetry, nor to play with their own children, nor even, in the end, to know very well where they are, nor even to know where the forest is, stones, dust, leaves, ponds, spring, summer - where life and death are...

I'd like to think that in some way I could recover the happiness of my youth: the happiness in which "design" or art - so-called art - was life itself, and in which life was art - by which I mean creativeness, the knowledge of being part of the planet and of the living history of the people around us...And I'd like it if there were no more talk about the fortunate and unfortunate, of better and worse, of those who are artists and those

The Palevsky house in Malibu, 1984-85, presents a relatively austere setting that can calmly accommodate classical sculpture and Pop art.

who are not; if instead they talked about things to do together, about the things we are surely all capable of doing, as we were capable of doing together many years ago... I should like to find a place where, together, people could try and make things with their hands or with machines, or any other way, not as boy scouts nor even as craftsmen, or workers, or even less as "artists", but as men with arms,legs, hands, feet, hair, sex, saliva, eyes and breath – and to make those things not to possess them and keep them, not even to give them to others, but to see what has to be done, to make certain things - that is, to try to make them, to see whether all of us can make things, other things, with our hands or machines or whatever else. Can it be tried?'
(Ettore Sottsass 1973, quoted in *Sottsass's Scrapbook*, Casabella 1976)

acknowledgements

As the bibliography of this book shows, a number of excellent articles, books and exhibition catalogues about Italian design in general and the work of Sottsass in particular have been published in the last twenty years. All of them have been helpful and illuminating. But like all contemporary writers on Sottsass I am particularly indebted for inspiration and information to Barbara Radice, whose writing on Memphis and Sottsass Associates are based on close personal involvement and understanding. My greatest debt is to Ettore Sottsass himself who was characteristically generous with his time and ideas and who continues to reassure us that he is entirely deserving of the title of design hero.

The publishers particularly acknowledge the help of Sottsass Associates, Memphis and Olivetti in the provision of photographs, and thank the following photographers: Studio Azzurro, Aldo Ballo, Occhio Magico, Santi Gallega, Peter Ogilvie, Tom Vack and others.

bibliography

Selected books on Italian Design

Ambasz, E. *Italy: The New Domestic Landscape*, New York, 1972
Branzi, A. *The Hot House: Italian New Wave Design*, London, 1984
Design Process Olivetti 1908-1983, Ivrea, 1984
Gregotti, V. *New Directions in Italian Architecture*, London, 1968
Heisinger, K.B. & Marcius, G.H. *Design since 1945*, London, 1983
Kicherer, S. *Olivetti*, London, 1990
Radice, B. *Memphis: the New International Style*, Milan, 1981
Radice, B. *Memphis: Research, Experience, Result, Failures and Success of New Design*, New York, 1985
Sartago, P. *Italian Re-Evolution: Design in Italian Society in the Eighties*, La Jolla, 1982
Sparke, P. *Italian Design 1870 to the Present*, London, 1988

Selected books & catalogues on Ettore Sottsass & Sottsass Associates

Di Castro, F. *Sottsass Scrapbook*, Milan, 1976
Radice, B. *Ettore Sottsass, Design Metaphors*, Milan, 1987
Radice, B. *Sottsass Associates*, Milan & New York, 1988
Sparke, P. *Ettore Sottsass Jnr.*, London, 1982
Ettore Sottsass Jnr., de l'objet fini à la fin de l'objet, CCI Paris, 1976
Ettore Sottsass Jnr., Israel Museum, 1976

Selected articles on Sottsass in English

Best, A. 'For the Archetypal Woman', *Design* no 249, London, 1969
Best, A. 'Medium Cool Message', *Design* no 262, London, 1970
Best, A. 'Of Machines and Men',*Design* no 237, London, 1968
J.R.G. 'Turning On', *Industrial Design*, New York, July 1970
'Sottsass, Superstudio, Mindscapes', *Design Quarterly*, Minneapolis, 1973
Sparke, A. 'A Peasant Genius', *Design*, London, June 1981
Sudjic, D. 'Sottsass & Co.', *Crafts*, London, November 1987
Waterhouse, R. 'A Valentine for Your Thoughts', *Design* no 250, London, 1969

Selected articles by Sottsass in English

Introduction to *Catalogue for Decorative Furniture in Modern Style 1979-80, Milan, 1980*

'Could Anything be More Ridiculous?', *Design* no 262, London, 1970
'Experience with Ceramics', *Domus* no 489, Milan, 1970
'Conversations with Designers', *Design*, London, January 1974
'Block Notes', *Casabella* no 408, Milan, 1975